HOW TO READ HANDS

A fascinating guide to the ancient art of hand analysis, revealing reliable methods of character interpretation

HOW TO
READ HANDS

by

LORI REID

THE AQUARIAN PRESS
Wellingborough, Northamptonshire

First published April 1985
Second Impression June 1985

British Library Cataloguing in Publication Data

Reid, Lori
  How to read hands.
  1. Palmistry
  I. Title
  133.6   BF921

  ISBN 0-85030-431-8

*The Aquarian Press is part of the
Thorsons Publishing Group*

Printed in Great Britain by
Richard Clay (The Chaucer Press) Ltd.,
Bungay, Suffolk

I should like to thank all my dear friends and loved ones who have helped me throughout the writing of this book.

I particularly wish to show my gratitude to Derek and Julia Parker for their constant encouragement and especially to Julia for so kindly contributing the foreword. Also to 'Marcia Gray' for allowing me to publish her personal hand analysis.

I dedicate this book to Chris and Fraser.

CONTENTS

FOREWORD

I first met Lori Reid in the 1970s, when we were appearing together in a series of BBC television programmes — she as palmist, I as astrologer. From the very barest information which could enable us to produce a character analysis, we were talking about personalities previously unknown to us, and they were later commenting on our work.

Until then, I had considered palmistry an interesting discipline, but probably a far less searching, incisive and constructive one than astrology! It could not, I thought, help an individual to the full realization of his or her potential, assess psychological motivation or personal difficulties as accurately as my own subject.

Fascinatingly, we found that week after week Lori and I, without conferring, would arrive at the studio with almost identical findings set out in our respective scripts! Watching her at work, I was impressed to see that, in her hands, palmistry was no more gypsy-fortune-telling mumbo-jumbo than (I hope) astrology is in mine.

Apart from serving as a general introduction to the subject, this book sets out palmistry not only as an important aid to personal development, but an extremely worthwhile counselling technique. There is no more rewarding activity than helping others to find greater self-fulfilment, or even just to iron out some of the complications in their lives — while none of us can fail to profit from greater realization of what makes us individual, makes us *us*.

Hand analysis, as Lori calls it, thus avoiding what has become a faintly pejorative term, is obviously a study which can profit us all, and her approach to her subject is one which is entirely relevant to the twentieth century. Yes, she respects the traditions of her craft and art, but combines those traditions with the latest techniques, and with her own experience and enthusiasm. Her book is scholarly without being dull, readable without being shallow. It is the best possible introduction to an engrossing subject. And yes, it's also fun!

JULIA PARKER

PART ONE

The Basics

CHAPTER ONE

Hand Analysis

What is Hand Analysis?

When you ask most people to describe hand analysis the most usual reply is that it's something like 'fortune telling by reading the lines on the palms of the hands'. In fact, hand analysis is a complex investigative process, a piece of detective work, by which information about an individual is slowly put together through the careful and meticulous study of his or her hands. The study itself is conducted on several levels — no one factor stands alone — each part modifies, confirms and corroborates every other until a profile of the individual is built up.

The first level that must be analysed is the shape of the hand itself. This lays down the basic character and together with the actual structure and formation of the palm and fingers, the nails, the colour, the texture and even the temperature must be assessed at this stage.

The next step is to look at the skin markings and to superimpose this information onto the first level. When considering the skin markings, not only the well-known and easily recognizable finger prints are looked at, but the entire skin patterning which covers the whole of the palm is examined in detail. The modern name for the finger prints and all other patterns created by the actual skin ridges is dermatoglyphics.

Next, the way the hands are held and the stance of the fingers are both observed. It is now widely accepted that gesture is an important clue to personality and make-up and, even if the hand is not being examined in the flesh but only in a print form, the way it has been placed on paper, the stance of the fingers and the relation of the thumb to the palm must all be taken into consideration at this point.

Finally, it is time to look at the lines, to examine in detail both course and structure. By thus superimposing this information onto the rest, a clear picture of the individual should emerge.

So, a quick checklist of the levels of the investigative procedure for a good analysis of the hand looks like this:

1.   The shape of the hand (nails, colour, texture).
2.   Dermatoglyphics (finger prints, skin patterns).
3.   Gesture (the way the hand and fingers are held).
4.   The lines (course and structure).

Popular Misconceptions

I feel it is important here to try to dispel some of the myths and old wives' tales that surround the study of the hand. The most popular misconception that our 'fate' is irrevocably engraved in our hands is, I'm glad to say, fast dying a death. Many people now readily acknowledge that the lines on their hands change, for they are able to observe this phenomenon for themselves over the course of years. Indeed, the lines can, and do, change and sometimes quite quickly so as in the case of stress and tension lines on the finger tips. These changes in the lines take place according to our experiences, influences and relationships in life which colour our understanding and perspective; our conscious decisions, positive thinking, changes of environment and life-styles, states of mind and health all contribute their own subtle patterns in our hands. This all goes to prove that we are not 'stuck with our destinies', as so many people used to believe, but that, as living, thinking, feeling human beings we have the power not only to choose but also to make our own destinies for ourselves.

Essentially, the hand is a useful guide to the understanding of our character and personality and it acts as an indicator of the possibilities and future events that are likely to touch our lives. But what we must always be aware of is that we possess free will and, as such, we can decide for ourselves whether to develop the potential that is shown, whether indeed to accept blindly any of the future prospects or to actively intervene.

For instance, if there were any future trends shown that perhaps we did not like the look of, it is conceivably possible that we might be able to steer clear of that whole set of circumstances, we might indeed be able to skirt around those events or obviate them from happening altogether. If the events shown were completely unavoidable, then at least we would be prepared for them and thus better able to handle all the implications as they appear to us. Equally so, the hand can alert us to opportunities and possibilities which we may never have thought about and by choosing to develop and explore these events we would find that the patterns in our hands would change accordingly.

Another misconception I often hear concerns the right and left hands and I'll bet you've heard it too: 'the left hand is what you're born with and the right is what you make of yourself.' This is utter rubbish — but there are significant differences between the two which should be explained. Around 13 per cent of people in Great Britain are born left-handed. It's really only in recent years that we have been able to get the true statistics on this because in the past left-handers were considered unnatural and great lengths were taken to make those poor unfortunates conform to the norm. I've heard countless gruesome stories of people who were forced to sit with their left hand tied behind their backs in order to force them to use their right. And for all we know, this may still be going on in some places!

Recent studies in right- and left-handedness have been carried out and have shown that the hands correspond to the right and left hemispheres of the brain. Interestingly, each hemisphere carries out unique functions. The left deals with the more hard-core functions of logic, writing, speech, maths, reading and lots more which we might call masculine-orientated subjects. The right hemisphere deals with what might be known as the softer, more feminine-orientated matters such as creativity, art, intuition, emotions, music, etc. What then happens, as Figure 1 shows, is most fascinating because the messages from each half of the brain are crossed over so that the right hemisphere dominates the left side of the body and the left hemisphere the right side of the body.

Because the messages are crossed over it is the right hand, then, which represents the functions of the left brain hemisphere and the left hand which represents the functions of the right hemisphere. So, when analysing the hands it is the right hand which tells us about the individual's objective, conscious self, the persona, in fact, and the left hand which reveals the subjective, subconscious side or anima. On a left-hander, it is a simple case of reversal because the functions of

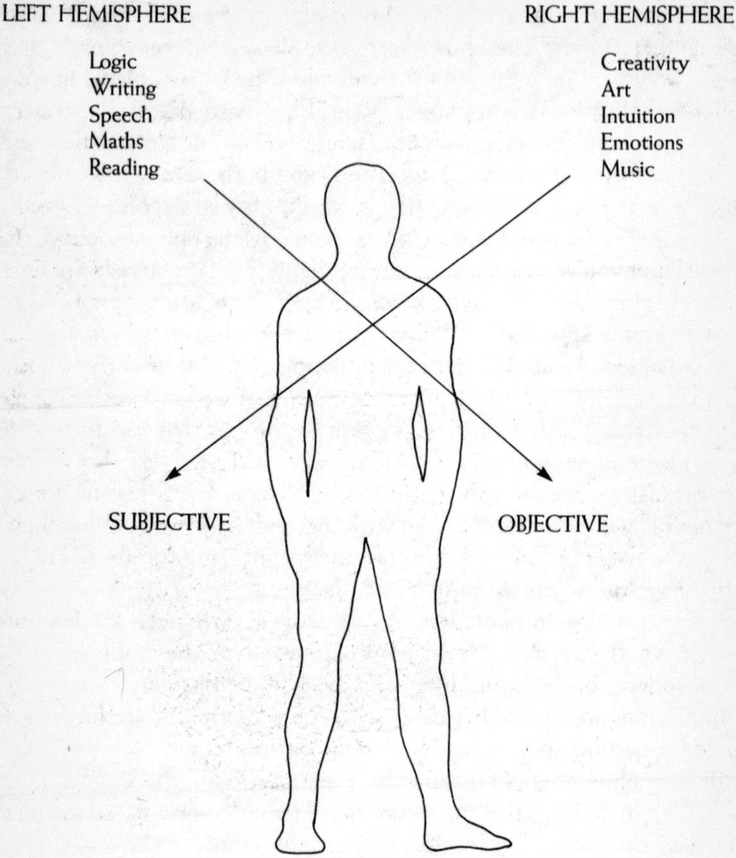

LEFT HEMISPHERE   RIGHT HEMISPHERE

    Logic   Creativity
    Writing   Art
    Speech   Intuition
    Maths   Emotions
    Reading   Music

SUBJECTIVE   OBJECTIVE

Figure 1

the hemispheres are reversed so that we look to the left as the objective
hand and the right as the subjective one.

A third misconception I tend to hear frequently is that the lines on
our hands are formed through the everyday movements we make or
through the requirements of our jobs. Again, this is nonsense. The
major lines are traced onto the hands sometime between the 13th and
15th weeks of foetal development and a new-born baby already has
a fine system of lines at birth. That our jobs create the lines for us

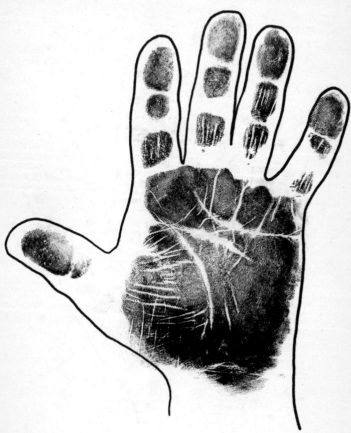

Figure 2a

is equally wrong for I have seen many people whose occupations make little demand on their manual dexterity and who have extremely lined hands whereas some manually skilled workers have very few lines indeed. Figures 2a and 2b illustrate this point beautifully. The prints belong to two men who are both in their 50s, one has been in manual work since he was 12 years old and the other belongs to a man who works as a representative for a large company. What is interesting is that it is Figure 2a, the hand which has only the main lines, which

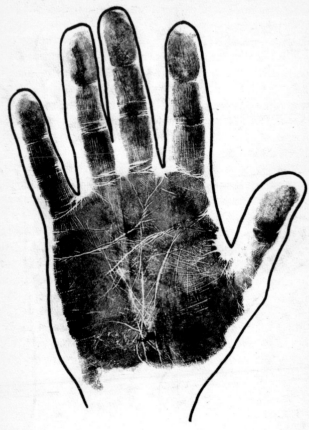

Figure 2b

belongs to the manual worker, whereas Figure 2b, the hand with many more lines, belongs to the representative!

What Does Hand Analysis Tell Us?

A good analysis of the hand can give us a wealth of information about ourselves. For a start, it can clearly reveal our character traits, our attitudes, behaviour, motivation and the way we think. It can give us valuable insights into the way we relate to other people and it gives us an understanding of our expectations of those relationships — both romantic and otherwise!

Looking at our hands can explain our potential, our innate gifts and talents and those inherited qualities that are lying dormant and ready to be developed. Our general state of mind and, equally importantly, our state of health can be clearly shown up so that we can take the necessary action to improve our situation as the case may be. Finally, the hand can give us important clues about the possible opportunities, events or the outcome of the actions and decisions which we are likely to make in the future.

There are serious applications for hand analysis in both the psychological and medical fields. In the psychological field, hand analysis would be a superb aid to the understanding of personality and motivation and it could certainly help to sort out individual problems and behavioural complexities. In the medical field, hand analysis could be used as an invaluable diagnostic tool. In fact, a lot of research is currently being carried out in America and Europe alike which is showing certain correlations between skin patterns and chromosomal abnormalities such as Down's Syndrome, for example, and it is quite conceivable that the hand could be used as a simple tool in genetic counselling in the future. Certainly, doctors already look at the hand for a variety of clues in their diagnoses of disease but there is still so much scope and much, much more research needs to be done in these areas.

How Does it Work?

I am often asked how hand analysis works and why indeed should our characters be mapped onto our hands anyway. There's a very simple answer to this one, and that is: no one really knows. This whole question is open to speculation and the only way I can attempt to explain it is that there must be some kind of connection between our body chemistry and the natural electrical impulses we emit which imprint various patterns, not only on our hands, but also on other parts of our bodies. It is certainly true that there is a vast concentration of nerve endings on our palms and so possibly this makes the hand an easy base on which to print these patterns. It's only because the hand has been studied for countless thousands of years that we have built up a system of knowledge which works, but I'm quite convinced that, if we were capable of interpreting the patterns, we would find information just as valuable imprinted elsewhere on the body.

That our body chemistry should be responsible for printing such information on our hands is not quite so far-fetched as it sounds when we consider some of the other oddities that go on in our bodies — often without us even knowing about them. Consider, for instance, some of the symptoms which are recognized pointers to disease: yellowing eyeballs as an indicator of jaundice; hair loss and bulging eyes in cases of hyperthyroidism; and what about all those odd allergic reactions which, even now, can't be fully explained? Why on earth, we might indeed ask, should a complaint of the liver produce yellow eyeballs and why should eating sea-food, for example, bring some people out in a rash as if they had just run through a field of stinging nettles? Unless we know and understand the body mechanisms these seemingly unconnected symptoms must surely seem very odd indeed. And so, too, does it seem odd that patterns of our lives should be somehow transmitted to and inscribed in our hands but it is only because we don't know how it works that is appears so strange. If we did know, if we had a neat scientific explanation for it, then I'm sure it would all seem so simple, so plausible, so logical and obvious. We mustn't fall into the trap of rejecting the phenomenon of hand analysis simply on the grounds that we as yet have no scientific explanation for it.

A Question of Conduct

It must always be borne in mind that hand analysis is a powerful tool and that the analyst is in a position of power and authority. I am ever mindful of this power and go to great pains never to abuse my position when dealing with others. Most people I meet are fascinated by the whole subject of the study of the hand and they are invariably eager to hear something about themselves, often spontaneously proffering their hand to me for a quick glance. The unwary analyst could do untold damage even in this most informal of situations for the subject is open and ready to receive and probably accept whatever is going to be said about him or herself. The wrong deduction or the unguarded statement could have far-reaching consequences on that subject's life which the analyst may never ever know about and yet be completely responsible for. What we must always remember is that it is so easy to sow the seed of suggestion in the mind, thereby perhaps leading the subject, even the most staunchly cynical, to reflect upon it at a later, more vulnerable moment.

So, it is vitally important always to be sure that the basic information is correct, to be always aware of self-fulfilling prophesies, to explain about the subject's own power of freewill and possibility of change in the hand. The subject should, in this way, be reassured at all times, and guidance should be given on turning any negative qualities or events into positive attributes and actions.

CHAPTER TWO

The Outline

Taking a Simple Outline

Much valuable information about an individual can be gleaned just by looking at the simple outline of the hand alone long before even beginning to consider any markings on the palm itself. At this stage

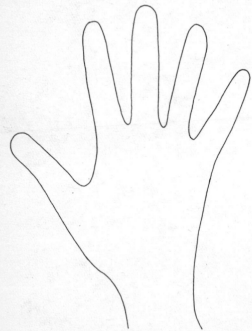

Figure 3

it is essential for the hand to be placed on the paper in as natural a pose as possible because, as will soon become apparent, what we will be looking at here is the relationship between the fingers and thumb, their relative lengths and how they are held in relation to each other.

So, in order to take a good outline, ask the individual concerned to first of all shake both hands to loosen them up and then to place them comfortably on a sheet of paper. Trace, with a fine pencil point, all around the palm, including about 2-3cm of the wrist, to end up with an outline as illustrated in Figure 3. It is important to get an accurate tracing of the fingertips and here long nails can sometimes create a problem so in this case it might sometimes be possible to draw around the finger underneath the nail or, if not, then try to copy the shape of the tip once the hand has been lifted off the page.

The Fingers

There are at least three ways of naming the fingers (Figure 4).

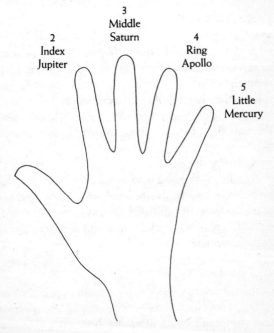

Figure 4

Firstly, they can be referred to by their most common names of index, middle finger, ring finger and little finger. Secondly, they can be anatomically classified as digits 1, 2, 3, 4 and 5 but care must be taken here because digit 1 specifically refers to the thumb so that digit 2 becomes the index and so on. Thirdly, the fingers may be known by their classical names of Jupiter, Saturn, Apollo and Mercury. These classical connotations are merely a form of shorthand by which the principles that are represented by each individual finger are quickly recognized.

Jupiter or the index finger

In classical mythology, Jupiter was the chief god and ruler of the world. As applied to hand analysis, this finger is basically known as the 'me' finger and represents the ego, the conscious self in the environment and how the individuals see themselves or their standing in the world. Additionally, it tells us something about the individual's socio-political awareness and, as such, often stands for religion, politics and the law.

Saturn or the middle finger

Saturn was the mythological father of Jupiter and so has become associated with old age and contemplative study. For our purposes, this finger represents the wherewithal to live, anything to do with the basic essentials of life including property, mining, agriculture, management, the household in general and husbandry. Very importantly, the middle finger represents the individual's idea of security although it can also give an insight into study and research.

Apollo or the ring finger

In legend, Apollo was the god who drove the sun in his golden chariot across the heavens and was associated with music and poetry, with prophecy and healing. In hand analysis this finger represents anything connected with creativity and the arts and it reveals the individual's inner sense of happiness and fulfilment.

Mercury or the little finger

Mythologically, Mercury was the messenger of the gods and giver of sleep. Because of his classical role the finger of Mercury has now come to represent communications, literature, business and medical science.

Interestingly, it can also reveal much about the individual's sexual and subconscious drives.

Length of Fingers

When determining whether the fingers are long or short, it is the middle one which is used as the gauge. The average length for this finger should be around ¾ to ⅞ the total length of the palm. Any longer than this then the fingers can be considered as long and, conversely of course, any shorter and the fingers are considered as short.

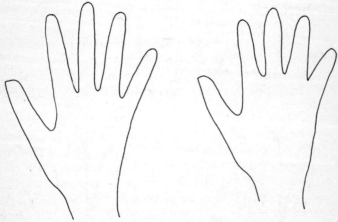

Figure 5   Figure 6

The longer the fingers the more patient and painstaking the individual (Figure 5). People who possess long fingers can sit for ages poring over fine, intricate and elaborate work. They can be meticulous with an eye for detail and needing time to think, to ponder and to ruminate and because of this may be considered as rather slowish types. These people would make fine craftsmen, mathematicians, logicians and they are to be found in any occupation requiring concentration and careful, thorough detailed work.

Short fingers instantly denote impatience especially with detail and minutiae (Figure 6). Anything to do with frustrating red-tape and pedantic nit-picking would rankle. People with short fingers are the impulsive, instinctive and intuitive types. They go for the overall view rather than homing in on the detail and they are excellent at making plans and initiating projects, preferring to leave the finer points to their longer-fingered colleagues whilst they themselves move on to the next project in hand. Don't ever expect short-fingered people to go by the rule book — this is much too slow for them; and don't be surprised if you find that they can't suffer fools gladly either! Because of the speed at which they pick up and process information, these people are excellent as organizers, administrators and project planners, especially in any situation where they can work with others.

Finger Settings

The way the fingers are set on the palm is important to note. When the fingers form a gentle curve above the palm, as seen in Figure 7, this is considered a normal setting and shows a well-balanced individual, one who does not live by extremes and who has moderate and tolerant views.

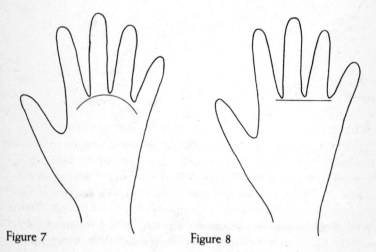

Figure 7   Figure 8

If, as in Figure 8, the fingers are set in a straight and even line, these individuals can be so self-confident that they may be in danger of being arrogant. These people may have plenty of drive and can be a bit pushy and even aggressive at times. Because there are few self-doubts, people with this straight setting generally believe that whatever they do must be right!

Individuals whose first and fourth fingers are especially low-set in comparison to the middle one are usually the types who are thought to have a 'chip on their shoulder', mainly due to an inferiority complex and to a lack of trust and belief in themselves coupled with a lack of self-confidence (Figure 9).

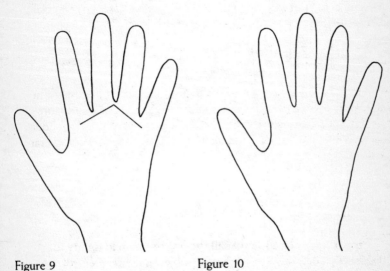

Figure 9   Figure 10

When it is only the little finger which is noticeably low-set (Figure 10), it reveals a fundamental lack of self-confidence. This lack of self-confidence, however, is not something which is a character defect *per se* of the individual but it is, rather, due to early environmental or parental conditioning. For instance, it might have occurred because, as children, these individuals felt that they had to constantly strive to meet their parents' expectations. Another example might be that youngsters feel they have to compete with older and, perhaps, brighter brothers and sisters. Or possibly the children simply didn't fit in with their family philosophy or background. Any of these sorts of examples would result in those individuals growing up with a strong lack of confidence and lack of faith in their abilities.

Finger Spacings

It is important, when taking a print or an outline, that the hand should be placed on the paper in as comfortable a position as possible. In this way the fingers will fall into a natural stance and form a pattern which can then be interpreted.

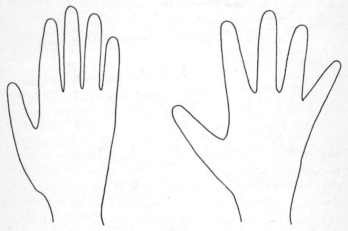

Figure 11   Figure 12

If the hand is placed so that all the fingers are held tightly together (Figure 11), it may be assumed that the subject is rather reserved, possibly introverted and of the fairly dependent type. There's a sense of restriction and limitation of expression here so that one feels that these subjects are 'holding themselves in'.

When the fingers are all spaced out (Figure 12), the subject is fairly open and extroverted. These people are usually vivacious and alert, the outgoing, optimistic, happy-go-lucky types who are never afraid of speaking their mind or talking about their feelings.

If the index finger falls away from the rest and thus forms a wide space between itself and the second finger this shows intellectual independence (Figure 13). With this formation the individuals like to think for themselves, to formulate their own conclusions from past experiences rather than from hearsay or what they are told by the media.

A rather unusual formation is when the middle and ring fingers are

Figure 13

Figure 14

held apart (Figure 14). Invariably, this indicates resourcefulness on the part of the individual. These people often need time on their own; perhaps they are better at working by themselves as 'back room men and women' rather than in groups or with others. Certainly, they need time on their own to 'recharge their batteries' and refresh their minds and, because of this, they may be considered as loners or somewhat anti-social.

Figure 15

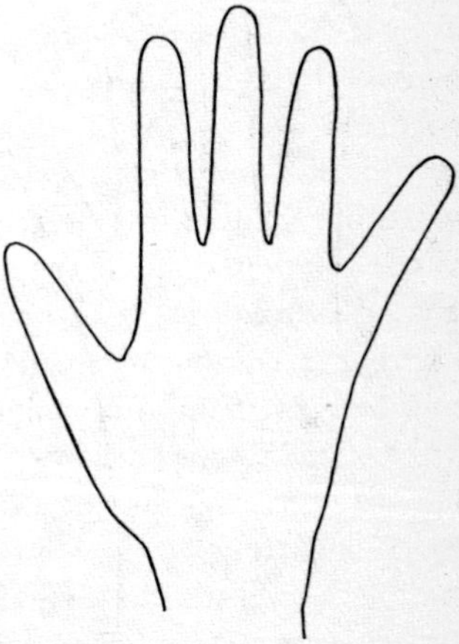

Figure 16

Conversely, when the middle and ring fingers are held together (Figure 15), it shows a need for security. People who display this pattern usually value and enjoy the company of others but domestic peace and harmony is of paramount importance to them. Sometimes, when only the tips of these two fingers point towards each other it can show a feeling of guilt, of divided loyalties, between domestic duty and the need for personal career satisfaction and gratification.

When the little finger is held widely apart from the rest (Figure 16), it is a sign of the need for physical independence and personal freedom to come and go as the individual chooses. People with this formation can so easily feel trapped if they think that their movements are in any way restricted, if they feel hemmed in or that their 'wings have been clipped'.

Finger Joints

Some people have very smooth fingers (Figure 17), whilst others have noticeably protuberant joints (Figure 18). Smooth-fingered folk are generally of the inspirational kind for their ideas come and go almost without needing any processing. Because of this they can be categorized as impressionable.

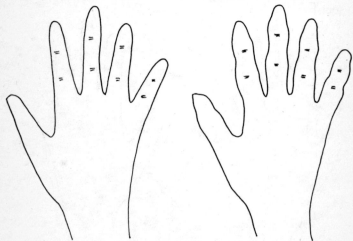

Figure 17   Figure 18

When both the top and bottom joints are protuberant these are known as knotted fingers and imply a philosophical turn of mind. Such people need to take time to think things out, especially when they are faced with making decisions or when they have a problem to sort out. Never expect these people to respond instantly — they really do need time to reflect, to consider and to analyse their thoughts before formulating their answers.

If only the basal joints are pronounced whilst the top ones are smooth then this denotes a person who needs a tidy and ordered environment in which to live and work.

The Thumb

The thumb is a uniquely human development and provides much insight into character and personality. Ideally, this digit should look balanced and in harmony with the rest of the hand. It represents will-power and drive together with reason and logic. Too small, weak or thin in comparison to the rest (Figure 19), and the individual lacks strength of character. Over-large, heavy or bulbous in relation to the fingers and palm (Figure 20), would denote someone who is perhaps forceful, over-dominant and aggressive.

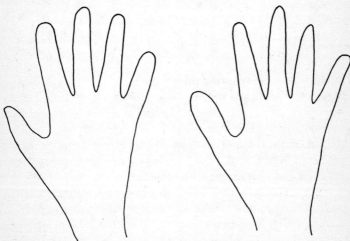

Figure 19   Figure 20

Angle of Opening

The angle at which the thumb opens away from the palm is most significant. Oriental philosophy maintains that a thumb which opens out to 90 degrees shows harmony of mind, body and spirit. The norm, though, is for a thumb to form an angle of between 45 and 90 degrees (Figure 21), and this would denote a confident, easy-going, sunny disposition, a good blend of introversion/extroversion and a generally well-balanced mentality.

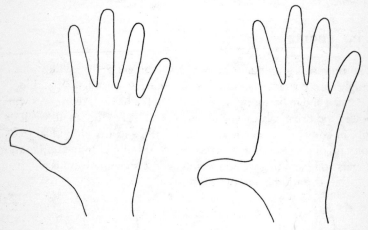

Figure 21   Figure 22

Those who can easily spread their thumbs to more than 90 degrees are extremely extroverted and even uninhibited (Figure 22). They are the non-conformist types, often adventurous and possibly too open for their own good. These people lack concentration and are all too easily distracted at the drop of a hat. What's more, this is the sign of extravagance. Never send these people out shopping with an open cheque book and without a specific shopping list for they won't come home with the essentials but rather with a basket full of luxuries, which although most enjoyable, won't do much for the housekeeping!

An angle which is formed of around 45 degrees or less highlights a more introverted and inhibited nature (Figure 23). These people are persistent and able to concentrate for long periods at a time. They

Figure 23

tend to be reserved, keeping themselves to themselves. Often they have rather fixed ideas and, according to the degree of tightness, they may be narrow-minded and even bigoted. The tighter the angle, the more intensity, control and self-restraint is implied.

Sometimes, individuals may hold their thumbs in an extremely acute angle when they are suffering from anxiety and stress. This temporary measure, when they are afflicted with problems, seems to point to a time of added concentration, a time when they are imposing great self-control, when they are mustering their resources and reappraising their situation. As the problems are resolved, so a more relaxed pose for the thumb is adopted.

It is vital always to check both hands for discrepancies as this is where hand-analysis becomes so very complex and fascinating. If, on right-handed individuals, the right thumbs form a tighter angle than the left ones then, *either,* this illustrates a temporary crisis of stress and anxiety, *or,* these people have somehow been forced, through maturity, to conform or to impose tighter controls on themselves. If, conversely, the right thumbs are held at a wider angle than the left ones, this would directly show a rather restrictive upbringing — either because of financial difficulties, sickness, bigoted parents, or whatever — and it is through independence, maturity or a different environment that these people have been able to flourish and fully develop their characters.

Thumb Settings

There is no really satisfactory explanation nor indeed any true clarity in literature regarding the setting of the thumb. Generally, a thumb which is set high on the hand seems to form a much more acute angle to the palm whilst one which is set lower down seems to naturally open out much wider. So it would seem fair to assume that a high-set thumb denotes a more introverted and introspective person, whereas the lower the setting the more extroverted and expansive the individual.

Angularities of the Thumb

If the top joint of the thumb is markedly pronounced (Figure 24a), it denotes stubbornness even to the point of bloody-mindedness.

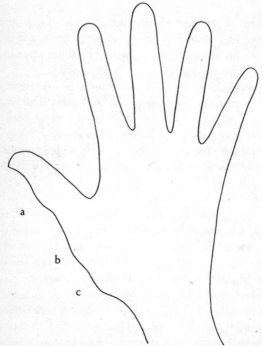

Figure 24

When the basal joint of the thumb is pronounced (Figure 24b), it is known as the angle of manual dexterity. This is invariably found on those who are good at using their hands for it reveals nimble fingers so DIY and handicrafts of all sorts would suit.

If, at the wrist, the palm sweeps out into a sharp, well-defined angle, then this is known as the angle of rhythm and timing (Figure 24c). Such a formation as this is found on the hands of those who have a good ear for music, and who often play a musical instrument themselves. Alternatively, it denotes a keen sense of timing, if not for music then possibly for sports, for delivering a punchline just at the right moment or even for arriving at one's destination at the exact appointed time.

The Percussion Edge

Working around the outline from the fingers, thumb and base of the hand we arrive at the percussion edge or ulna, as it is sometimes called.

Starting at the top, if the edge of the palm under the little finger noticeably bulges outwards (Figure 25), it can be said that these people live on their nerves and are perhaps highly strung. They are 'mental fidgets' for they are forever thinking and planning ahead and almost

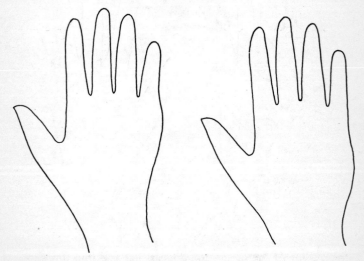

Figure 25   Figure 26

can't sit still for a minute without fretting or worrying over plans for the morrow. These people must take care not to let their minds drive their bodies too far, especially so if they are somewhat lacking in physical resources, as they may find that they just exhaust themselves both physically and mentally. Sound advice to these people is that they should try some tension-release or deep-breathing exercises, maybe even some simple yoga techniques in order to calm not only their bodies but also their minds.

If the whole percussion bows out from fingers to wrist (Figure 26), then this is the mark of creativity. Invariably, people with this formation are also highly intuitive and may even experience colourful and prophetic dreams. They should learn to listen and follow their instincts and inner feelings for these are an invaluable guide to their lives.

When the greatest development is seen lower down by the wrist (Figure 27), this highlights excellent physical resources and it is the sort of formation more typically seen on the hands of sportsmen and women — the active, energetic types who prefer the healthy, outdoor life.

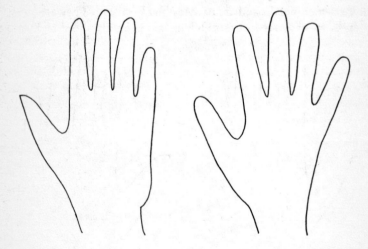

Figure 27   Figure 28

If the outline of the percussion appears flat and thin this shows a lack of physical stamina and staying power (Figure 28).

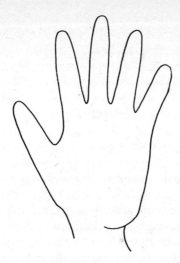

Figure 29

If, however, the whole of the ulna edge appears fuller and more generously endowed than any other part of the hand (Figure 29), then it is the subconscious or imaginative side of the individual that takes precedence over all other aspects of life. The development here reveals that it is the soul or creative side of the individual which matters most and which is far more important than anything material or worldly. Conversely, when the opposite, or thumb, side is more developed, then the dominant preoccupation in life revolves around the more concrete mundane and materialistic concerns of everyday living.

CHAPTER THREE

Looking at the Hand

When assessing the basic character of a person, there is nothing quite as revealing as an initial handshake. This provides a splendid opportunity not only to feel the texture and temperature of the hand but also to get an idea of the strength and robustness of the individual.

A thick, fleshy hand often denotes an earthy, materialistic type of person whereas a thin, wispy hand usually belongs to the ethereal, spiritual type. If the hand should feel springy and resilient to the touch it tells of an energetic person, someone who is healthy, with plenty of physical reserves and who might be considered the sporty type. A firm hand reveals a fairly tough, uncompromising and determined sort of person but a soft, flabby hand betrays the sensual, indolent type who rather likes a touch of the *dolce vita*.

The temperature of the hand should, of course, be judged according to the ambiance but a hand which is normally unusually cold suggests someone who is not very responsive or giving. A hot hand, though, reveals the spontaneous, impulsive and generous person, one who is always on the go with plenty of energy and enthusiasm in life. In between the two may be found the warm hand which, apart from representing the average temperature, also adds a fair degree of caution and a need for constant encouragement through life.

Of course, the temperature of the hand can also give a lot of clues regarding the individual's health. For instance, a hot hand, prone to perspiration, might be suggestive of thyroid activity or a very cold hand might imply circulatory problems. It is therefore important to make a mental note of these observations whilst not jumping to premature conclusions but waiting to add such findings to the rest of the analysis.

One last point whilst on the subject of temperature. Sometimes, a hand may feel cold to the touch and yet seems to radiate quite a lot of heat at a distance of, say, ten centimetres. If this is the case, and a medical stigmata is also present, then it is indicative of natural healing powers.

If the whole hand and fingers feel stiff and are held rather rigidly this tells of someone who tends to be inflexible, possibly dogmatic and unforthcoming. Supple, animated hands, however, usually belong to those who are flexible both in their disposition and outlook.

The Mounts

Some hands may feel fuller, warmer, fleshier or whatever, than others and this can be attributable to the little rounded lumps and bumps that cover the whole of the palm, as seen in Figure 30. These little fleshy pads are called the mounts, and their particular function is to cover and cushion the nerve endings and the blood vessels beneath

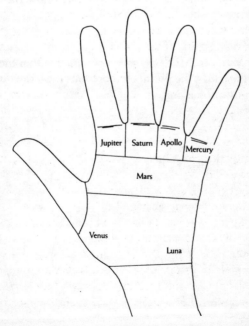

Figure 30

them. There are several of these, each one representing certain qualities according to its position on the palm and it is the way we express or bring to life those qualities which is portrayed in the appearance of the mount itself.

The mounts should, generally speaking, be springy — not too hard, nor too soft — and this applies especially so to the basal ones of Venus and Luna. Too soft and the person is a sensualist, a dreamer; too hard and we have someone who is a tough realist, someone who is pragmatic and phlegmatic in the extreme.

A good 'rule of thumb' to remember is that a high, well-shaped mount denotes quality vs. quantity, that is, integrity and discriminative tastes. A shapeless but large expanse, however, means quantity often at the expense of quality.

Some hand analysts hardly give any credence at all to the mounts but I, in fact, think they hold a great deal of information. To my mind it is extremely important to note which areas on the hand are more, and which less, developed as this will instantly show the subject's emphasis or stance in life.

The mount of Venus
The mount of Venus is that fleshy area contained within the life line and known as the ball of the thumb. It represents the individual's sense of being and gusto for living.

Figure 31   Figure 32

Full and round as in Figure 31, this mount reveals a vibrant, enthusiastic, outgoing nature. Those with this area well padded are full of life, virile, vital people. They are lively with plenty of energy and because of this they seem to bounce back fairly quickly after any physical ill health or emotional stress. As they possess a natural warmth, this makes them attractive to others, for they are very loving people, always prepared to give love but equally needful of being loved back.

If the mount is pale, flat and almost appears altogether non-existent as seen in Figure 32, it tells of a lack of vitality. It's as if the very spark of life is missing and the person can, at times, become quite morose. These people are not very physically robust, they have low energy levels and as such are open to illness without the recuperative strength seen in the former type. Some may indeed be rather wan and sickly, in fact. In addition, they can appear to be reserved and, possibly even, lacking in fundamental human warmth.

When the mount is springy to the touch it illustrates the lively, energetic, dynamic sort of person who is positively brimming with health and always prepared for action.

If this area feels rather flabby it is indicative of someone who likes an easy, soft life and who has a tendency to indolence. This is one of the principal signs of the sensualist.

The person who seems larger than life, who talks louder than everyone else, who eats more, who is more active and who exaggerates every aspect of life usually has such a huge mount of Venus that it appears completely out of proportion to the rest of the hand. In this case, in fact, the whole area would be the most dominant in the palm, noticeably overshadowing all the other mounts.

If in doubt as to the fullness of this mount, simply check the course of the life line skirting around it. For indications of good, healthy mental and physical well-being, the line should swing out clearly to the centre of the palm. If, however, the line should stick rather closely to the base of the thumb, thus not allowing much fullness to the mount, it reveals someone who is reserved, not very strong at all but with a strong tendency to a cynical disposition.

The mount of Luna
On the opposite side to Venus is found the mount of Luna. This is the area at the base of the percussion which lies just above the wrist.

The mount of Luna represents imagination, intuition and, generally, the subconscious. Those with a good mount here are the sensitive types, receptive to other people's moods, to impressions, to vibrations and to atmosphere. They seem to have a close rapport with, and an understanding of, Nature's rhythms and cycles. Above all, they are warm, sympathetic people who draw others to them because of their natural ability to empathize with and understand the human condition.

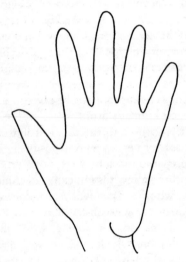

Figure 33

These qualities are all the more enhanced if the mount is located so low down on the palm that it sits well over the wrist (Figure 33). These folk are not only particularly sensitive to people's moods but can also get the feel of a place or a situation almost at a moment's glance. Sometimes dancers or those with an inherent sense of balance and poise can possess this formation too.

If the area rises to a high, pinkish dome, perception and perspicacity are the salient qualities of the individual. People with psychic powers invariably have this formation.

A large but soft and flabby mount typifies the dreamer, the person who has good intentions but who spends most of the time building castles in the air.

A flat, negligible mount of Luna tells of a total lack of imagination and describes a person of extreme conservatism with a conformist mentality.

The mount of Neptune

Between the mounts of Venus and Luna is situated the mount of Neptune. This, in fact, is not really a mount at all and very few people seem to have it developed to any degree. Although not much is, as yet, known about this area, it is believed that those who do have a rounded, well-formed mount here are the magnetic types. There's also the idea that they possess good, resonant voices and that they usually make excellent speakers. I have found that when this area is well-formed, the individual has a natural kindliness and seems able to generate a feeling of warmth and comfort.

If the area is especially wide and flat it can denote a total lack of self-reflection.

Upper Mars

The area of Upper Mars is found lying directly above the Luna mount and it represents moral courage, the subject's degree of tolerance, of persistence and resistance.

A well-developed area here, as illustrated by Figure 34, highlights

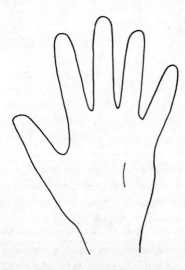

Figure 34

endurance in the face of difficulties; the spirit of the persecuted or of the martyr might be described in this way. Such people have strong moral principles and they would never turn their backs on their own beliefs or indeed on those in need. The people with amazingly high pain-thresholds invariably possess a well-padded mount here.

If the mount seems weak and lacking in substance then there is something missing in the moral fibre of that person. There may well be a lack of integrity and of loyalty and such people could indeed be called moral cowards. Tolerance to pain would also be rather low.

Lower Mars
The mount of Lower Mars is found above Venus and inside the top part of the life line. Whereas Upper Mars represents moral fortitude this mount tells of physical courage and prowess.

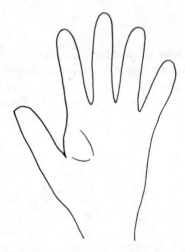

Figure 35

If this mount is over-developed so that it markedly forms a small hillock, it instantly reveals the argumentative, aggressive type (Figure 35). People with this type of formation love a challenge or a dare and they are ready to fight at the slightest provocation. The bigger this area, the more physical violence they possess and the best advice for them is to channel this energy into active sports and hard work-outs in order to get it out of their systems. A very large mount here, together with a short, thick thumb and weak head line, can pinpoint the out-and-out bully.

Under-developed, though, this area would show the weaker type of person, possibly the cowardly sort.

An average mount, one which appears in good proportion to the rest denotes the normal sort of determination and courage, without being foolhardy or defensively aggressive. These people will stand their ground, if need be, and this is another of the signs of the active, energetic, sporty type of person.

The plain of Mars

This is the area which bridges the gap between Upper and Lower Mars. It has become known as the reservoir of energy and the test here is to feel it between one's finger and thumb in order to gauge its depth and thickness.

If the whole area feels soft it is possible that the individual could be mean and selfish.

If thin, there may well be a lack of common sense and perhaps, too, it typifies the egocentric type of person.

A firm, thick, well-padded plain of Mars shows the resourceful, astute person who isn't easily 'taken in'.

But, flabby and soft, this area would highlight the lazy, self-indulgent people.

The mount of Jupiter

This mount lies directly below the index finger and it represents the ego, one's standing and sense of ambition in the world (Figure 36).

A normal, well-proportioned mount shows a fine sense of justice and high moral standards. A good amount of self-respect and self-esteem is necessary for a well-balanced life and this mount would portray these characteristics. Also, a sound understanding of one's strengths and weaknesses is seen here.

Should the mount be too high in comparison to the rest of the palm then it's possible that the owner could be arrogant, self-important and self-opinionated. Altogether, quite a pompous sort of person.

A very flat mount denotes the worrier, the person who tends to be easily led and at the mercy of the prevailing circumstances and environment.

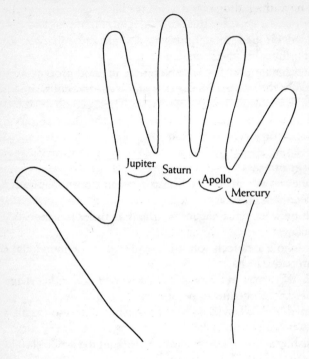

Figure 36

The mount of Saturn

This mount represents several diverse aspects of life: stability, property, the basic requirements for living, agriculture, sometimes study and philosophy, occasionally music too (Figure 36).

It is best if the mount of Saturn is not well-developed at all in the hand because when it is large or high it can indicate the gloomy, melancholy, pessimistic sort of person — the type who is known as a thorough wet blanket or a misery-guts. Such people can be solitary, unsociable types who go round spreading gloom and doom everywhere. Happily, this development is not often seen!

Sometimes, though, a little rounded mount can occur but here, instead of portraying the misanthropist, it can reveal the scholar and, especially so, the accomplished musician.

The mount of Apollo

The alternative name for this area is the mount of Sun and, as such, it conveys the message of creativity and artistry, of happiness and satisfaction (Figure 36).

A good, well-proportioned mount here suggests a warm, generous person with a sunny disposition. People whose mounts of Apollo seem fairly large are blessed with the sort of characters that tend to make them popular and attractive. They can be extroverts and usually rather fortunate types.

If the mount appears too large and out of balance with the rest then it tells of a showy, garish sort of person — a real 'flash Harry' — someone who is extravagant in life, who basks in attention and who falls prey to the least bit of flattery.

When this mount is deficient, though, it betrays frugality and practicality at the expense of beauty and comfort.

The mount of Mercury

This mount, under the little finger represents communications and personal expression (Figure 36).

A normal, well-balanced mount tells of a love of freedom and a hatred of restriction and limitation.

Large, the mount suggests nervous energy and a need for plenty of stimulation and challenge in life.

If flat and deficient, the mount reveals those who lack self-confidence, who are easily tongue-tied because they are always afraid of saying the wrong things lest they be laughed at or ridiculed in any way. These are the people who are generally rather shy and self-conscious.

But, if the mount seems to be well raised over a wide area, even encroaching into the territory of the Apollo mount, you can be sure that you have a garrulous person to contend with! This, indeed, is the principal sign of the chatterbox.

The Division of the Palm

The palm may be divided in two ways — vertically and horizontally — in order to establish which areas in life are the most salient or dominant to the subject.

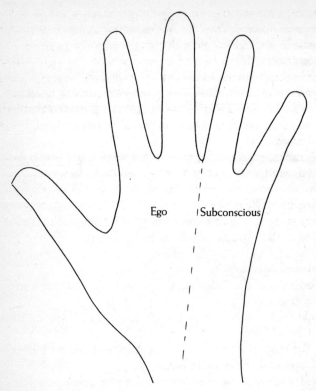

Ego | Subconscious

Figure 37

As illustrated in Figure 37, the vertical division may be drawn from between the Apollo and Saturn fingers straight down to the wrist. The cut-off point is made in this position because the boundaries created follow the course of the radial, median and ulna nerves. That part of the palm which lies on the radial, or thumb side, of the division represents the ego, the conscious self. The other half towards the percussion is known as the ulna side and it represents the subconscious, the instinctive side.

If, then, it is observed that the mounts of Venus, Lower Mars and Jupiter are in any way better developed than those on the percussion side, it can be said that the more conscious, logical, rational and positive aspects in life predominate.

If, on the contrary, the other side of the palm seems to have the greater development, then the person would possess more of the imaginative, sensitive and intuitive qualities in life.

The horizontal divisions can be made so that the palm is divided into three separate areas, as shown in Figure 38.

The basal part of the hand, just above the wrist, represents vital energy, physical strength and vitality. Here, in the mounts of Venus and Luna, can be seen the capacity for living, robustness and the body's physical resources.

If this part of the hand appears better developed than it is under the fingers then it denotes a strong, physical and energetic person, someone who tends to be earthy.

If, though, the palm tapers down towards the wrist so that this whole area appears weak, it reveals someone who is lacking in stamina, not

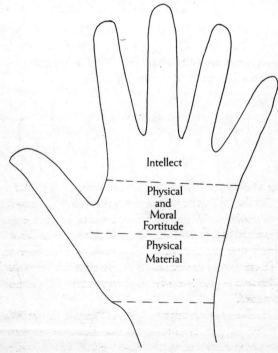

Intellect

Physical and Moral Fortitude

Physical Material

Figure 38

terribly physically strong and so who needs plenty of rest in order to conserve energy.

The central part of the palm represents staying power, physical courage, aggression, dare-devilry, together with moral integrity and fortitude. If it is this area which appears to be stronger than all the others then we have someone who is strong indeed in all these characteristics. Perhaps a true, brave, uncompromising leader of men, a Spartacus or a St Joan, might have had this sort of formation.

The band right across the palm, directly below the fingers, represents how we express ourselves creatively, spiritually and scientifically. So, if the whole palm opens out towards the fingers so that the greatest development is at the top, it indicates that intellectual pursuits and interests are predominant.

The Fingers

Turning the attention now higher up on the hand to the fingers, there are two points to observe at this stage. Firstly, as in Figure 39, notice whether the phalanges are full (what I refer to as podgy), or indeed, whether they are slim and firm, as shown in Figure 40.

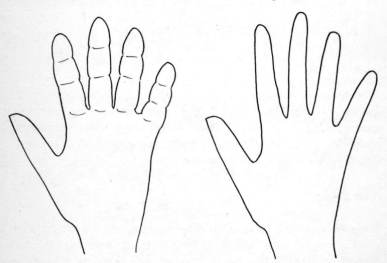

Figure 39   Figure 40

Full, rounded or podgy fingers, especially when this development is seen on the basal phalanges, usually signify an earthy or perhaps even a materialistic outlook. People with these kinds of fingers tend to be sensual, sometimes self-indulgent, and they enjoy all the comforts which make life softer and easier. The podgier the fingers, the more sensual and luxurious the subjects would like their lives to be.

The opposite to these are the thin, firm fingers. People with these types of fingers are more sparing, more frugal and more spiritual in outlook. They can exist quite happily without too many material chattels around them and they are able to tighten their belts philosophically when times are hard. These are the people who look for quality rather than quantity in their possessions and surroundings.

The second feature to look out for is the little rounded pad on the top phalanges which, when the finger is viewed from the side, looks like a drop of water hanging down and so is appropriately called a droplet (Figure 41).

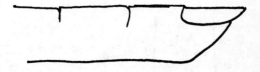

Figure 41

People with droplets on their fingers have a very sensitive touch and they are what I call tactile folk. They simply love the feel of different textures and can't resist touching anything in sight — fabrics, furnishings, prohibited museum exhibits, other people — they just find it extremely difficult to keep their hands to themselves!

The Nails

The nails provide a vast source of information, though mostly of a diagnostic nature and so will be dealt with in greater depth later on in the chapter on health. The shape, however, can give lots of clues to character and behaviour.

Most people would readily be able to make certain assumptions about an individual's character just by looking at whether the nails are manicured, dirty or bitten down to the quick. And indeed most of those assumptions would probably be quite correct. Beautifully manicured nails instantly give the idea of a fastidious, careful person whereas dirty nails suggest that less attention and importance is given to grooming and personal hygiene. Bitten nails, of course, imply a nervous, possibly even highly strung, individual.

Although these observations would also be made in passing when analysing a hand, far more important is the actual shape of the nail itself and, for this purpose, it is only the pink, growing part that is carefully considered.

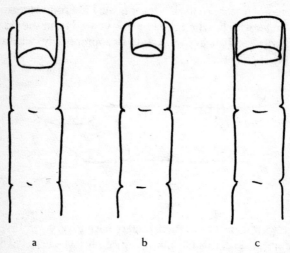

a   b   c

Figure 42

People with large nails which are squarish in shape (Figure 42a) tend to be fairly placid and they don't seem to rise to anger very quickly.

Smaller square nails (Figure 42b), suggest a cynical and critical view of life.

When a nail is oblong in shape, so that it is much wider than high (Figure 42c), it reveals a very quick temper. Stay away from such people when they are roused for they can explode with volcanic force! This is especially true when the oblong nail is found on the thumb. It must

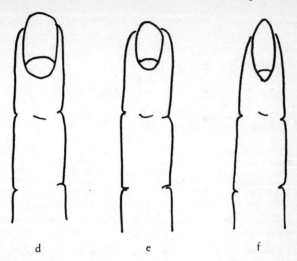

d　　　　　　　　e　　　　　　　　f

Figure 42 continued

be said, however, that at least with these types they don't sulk or smoulder for long but get their anger and frustration out in one fell swoop.

The long, filbert-shaped nail (Figure 42d), is associated with someone who is even-tempered and good-natured. Unlike the oblong nail, though, there is here a tendency in some to sulk, sometimes for long periods, when hurt or upset.

Short, rounded nails often indicate quick, intuitive powers (Figure 42e).

Almond-shaped nails (Figure 42f), tell of a gentle, easy-going nature. Such people tend to be refined but also seem to have a sensitive disposition.

Always remember that when assessing the nails, as with any other single feature on the hand, the information gleaned must be added to, confirmed, modified or corroborated by all other factors before the whole true picture of the individual concerned can emerge.

CHAPTER FOUR

Working from a Print

I find that when making a full analysis of a hand, working from a print is preferable by far to working on the actual hand itself. The main reason for this is that careful and painstaking attention can be focused on the print without receiving any confusing external stimuli from the individual. Invariably, too, much more detail emerges in the imprint and, of course, very accurate measurements can be taken and marked off against the image and the lines. Obviously, there are features which will be missed in this way, the colour and temperature of the hand itself, for instance, and so too, the shape and quality of the nails. But, if clear notes are made of these details at the time of taking the print then one can proceed with the analysis at leisure.

Taking a Print

There are several techniques and all sorts of inks or household products that can be used to take a good print. Finger-printing ink is sometimes recommended but this is often difficult to obtain and also needs solvents to clean the hands with afterwards. I find water-soluble lino printing ink is the best as this is simply washed off with soap and water. But even this may not be readily available and often needs to be ordered from good art shops. With a bit of ingenuity, though, it is possible to find things lying around at home which will do the job just as well and won't cost time, money and effort to obtain. Boot polish is one such handy household product and of course the one thing that almost everyone can fall back on is good old lipstick.

The professional way to take a print is to squeeze a little ink onto a sheet of glass and spread it thinly with a rubber roller. When the roller has been coated with the ink, run it all over the palm and fingers evenly, making sure that about a couple of centimetres of the wrist are inked up as well. If lipstick or boot polish are being used then a little will have to be rubbed on over the hand with a tissue or soft cloth. Then, ask the person to shake his or her hand for a moment in order to loosen it up and to place it, in as comfortable and as natural a position as possible, on a sheet of paper. The natural position is very important because lots of information can be gleaned from this. Once the hand is on the paper run a fine pencil all around it in order to draw in the outline.

That sounds simple enough but many people who have tried this for the first time will loudly declare that it's not at all as easy as that! For a start, applying the ink evenly is an art, even with the special inks, rollers and sheets of glass let alone trying to spread thick boot polish or lipstick. The first attempt may simply result in one great big splodge. Do persevere because, like all skills and techniques, this does take time to master and perfect. So, clean the hand and — try again.

The next little spot of bother that may be encountered is that the whole central part of the palm may not print at all. This is often the case when the surrounding mounts are well developed and the plain of Mars is thin or hollow. Take heart, even the professionals have trouble with this one. There are, of course, several methods for overcoming this little hurdle.

One way is to place the bottom edge of the sheet of paper on a rolling pin, rest the person's wrist on the base of the paper and slowly roll the hand back towards the body over the roller so that every part of the hand comes into contact with the paper. This sounds more complex than it actually is but, even so, it is a method which I don't personally like, or use, because it tends to distort the shape of the hand, it destroys any possibility of getting a natural pose and the outline has to be superimposed afterwards. However, in all fairness, there are those who do prefer this technique and who are able to obtain excellent results with it.

Rather, the method I use is to slip an ordinary table knife under the paper and press it up into the hollow of the palm. This is usually effective and most satisfactory but, if even this should fail, I place a wad of cotton wool under the paper and ask the person to cup the hand over that. Alternatively, turn the hand palm-side up and place the paper over it, pressing down into the hollow. Any of these methods, or indeed a combination of all of them, should finally do the trick. But do remember, though, that trial and error is the key and practice is the answer to obtaining clear prints which are good enough to get to work on.

Measuring Up

Once a good imprint has been taken, the next step is to carefully and accurately measure up the palms and fingers. This is an important exercise for several reasons. Firstly, measuring the palm helps to place it in its basic shape category. Secondly, the fingers are sometimes unevenly set so that they can appear unusually longer or shorter than they really are. Thirdly, the length of the individual phalanges must be worked out to ascertain which are predominant. And lastly, several

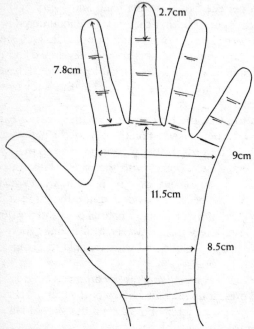

Figure 43

unexpected discrepancies of size and shape between right and left hands can sometimes emerge which may not be apparent at first glance and which make the analysis so much more complex and fascinating.

Following Figure 43, the first step is to measure the width of the palm both at the base just above the wrist, and at the top below the fingers. Next, measure the length from the top rascette (wrist 'bracelet' line) up to the bottom crease of the Saturn finger.

Now, measure each finger from the tip down to the bottom crease where each meets the palm. Finally, measure the individual phalanges, taking the measurements to the bottom crease line at every joint.

This should be done for both hands and the findings recorded at the side of the print. Having established the dimensions of the palm it is then possible to determine which shape category it belongs to.

Palm Shapes

It was in the nineteenth century that two eminent palmists, D'Arpentigny and Desbarolles, laid down some basic rules governing the shapes of hands. They believed that most hands fell into one of six categories which they called: elementary, square, spatulate, conic, philosophical and psychic. They added one more, which was a combination of two or more of these shapes, and called it the mixed hand.

Both D'Arpentigny and Desbarolles maintained that it is the shape of the hand which reveals the basic character of the individual. Indeed, this still holds true today and it is one of the fundamental principles on which an analysis is based. In fact, many modern hand analysts still adhere to these categories and apply them to each hand they see.

But, to expect hands, which are all unique, to fit neatly into any of these pure types is, in my opinion, a gross simplification of the complex art of hand analysis. True, most hands are instantly recognizable as being more of one pattern than another and thus pertaining to these categories but, to find a pure type which conforms exactly, is a difficult job indeed.

Personally, although I maintain some of these recognized and well-established categories, I prefer to separate the palms from the fingers. The reason for this is that all too often a palm may be characterized as, say, conic or spatulate, while the fingers belong more to the square or philosophical class. In this way, rather than treat the hand as a whole, thus invariably condemning it to the 'mixed' type, I deal first with the palm and then superimpose any extra information I discover concerning the fingers and likewise the thumb.

Bearing in mind the uniqueness and individuality of each palm, the categories I use are the square, the conic, the spatulate and the psychic. The philosophical classification I apply specifically to the fingers. It must, nevertheless, constantly be remembered that some palms may not match these discrete types but could be an amalgamation, in which case they would reveal a mixture of the character traits in each category concerned.

The square palm

The square palm (Figure 44) is so called because it is literally square in shape — it is as wide as it is long. People with square palms are basically practical, down-to-earth, pragmatic types. They are characterized by the fact that they are hard workers and, what they lack in imagination, they certainly make up for in practical expertise. They do work hard but in a plodding, systematic way, for they are steady and solid and they need their routine. In fact, they can become quite upset if their carefully planned routine gets unexpectedly disturbed. Generally, they are straightforward, level-headed folk with

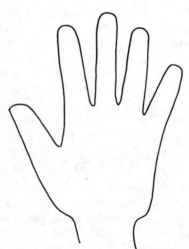

Figure 44

plenty of common sense. They can have an earthy turn of mind and certainly have their feet firmly planted on the ground. Respectable and law-abiding, they have a strong sense of discipline and authority and it is for this reason that so many square-palmed people are found in the police force or in the armed services. Most of them love to get out and about in the open air as much as possible and, if they are cooped up in an office all day — something which is anathema to a lot of them — they can't wait to get back to their gardens or stretch their legs on a long ramble.

Figure 45

There is a variation of the square palm which is oblong in shape (Figure 45). Although there are great similarities in the two, the people with the oblong palms tend to be more urbane and they prefer the indoor and more sophisticated interests rather than the rural or pastoral pursuits. The longer the palm, I find, the more the individual's tastes become refined.

The conic palm
The conic palm (Figure 46) tends towards a more rounded shape, often with a fairly well-developed percussion. This is a rather feminine hand

and highlights creative and artistic flair. People with this type of palm have a cheerful, optimistic outlook, and can be quite sensitive and intuitive, especially so if the percussion edge is bowed. They make excellent organizers but may have a tendency to impatience, particularly if the fingers are short. In this case they tend to work intuitively and may seem impulsive but they have the knack of 'catching on' for they are quick learners and quite adept at reading between the lines. They thrive on challenge and simply love to be in the sort of job where they have to be one step ahead all the time. Routine and a dead-end, 9-to-5 type of existence positively stultifies their enthusiasm and imagination. So, plenty of variety and change keeps them stimulated and vibrant. These people are at their best working with others or dealing with the general public and that is why any organizational, promotional or PR position would suit them well as would any occupation which requires a creative turn of mind, linguistic skills or artistic ability. Moreover, their adaptability means that they, more than any of the other types, can put up with all sorts of situations and environments and simply make the best out of them.

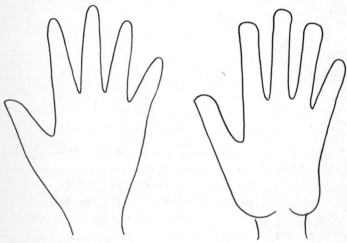

Figure 46   Figure 47

The spatulate palm
The spatulate palm (Figure 47) takes its name from the spatula shape,

sometimes narrow at the wrist and broadening out towards the fingers or, alternatively, wide at the base and tapering up to the top. Those who possess this type of palm are known as the doers, because of their energy, their vitality and their drive. If they aren't physically active then they are mentally on the go the whole time. It has been said that these are the inventors, the discoverers, the innovators and the initiators of ideas. Like the square-palmed folk they are active but, unlike them, they like to generate their own projects for they have extremely imaginative and inventive mentalities. Because of the richness of their imagination they are often characterized by their far-reaching ideas which can make them seem almost 'born before their time'. On the other hand, they may just be considered as eccentric, as dabblers or even as absent-minded professor types. Indeed, many scientists, explorers, missionaries and inventors have been known to possess this palm shape. But those who have the greatest development at the base, with the palm tapering up to the fingers, have so much physical energy that they are often amongst the best sportsmen and women of the country.

The psychic hand
The psychic palm (Figure 48) tends to be long and lean and yet has

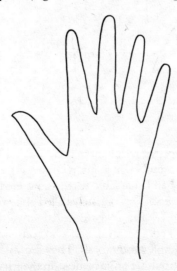

Figure 48

a wispy quality to it. This shape, because of its lack of robustness and lack of substance, tells of a fretful, anxious and highly strung nature. People with this type of palm can be extremely sensitive and, as such, become the poets, the dreamers, the visionaries amongst us. They have refined tastes, rarified even, with a strong sense for the aesthetics and, especially when long fingers accompany this palm, they can absorb themselves for hours on end in detail and minutiae. Because they seem to spend so much time with their heads in the clouds they are more spiritual than they are worldly and this makes them unrealistic and impractical, in fact, totally unsuited to the materialistic demands of everyday life. Impressionable and unpredictable, they must beware not to allow themselves to be easily led by stronger, more forceful types of people.

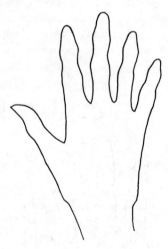

Figure 49

A variation of this type, when it is more bony and has long, knuckled fingers with extremely protuberant joints, is known as the philosophical hand (Figure 49). This hand characterizes the slow, meditative thinker and that is why it has been so appropriately called philosophical. People with this type of hand are the analytical, deductive thinkers, those who are the eternal seekers after truth and who constantly apply their minds to questions of ethics and morals. They are sticklers for detail and there is nothing impulsive or impetuous in their natures. Indeed, they can be frustratingly slow to respond to or formulate their opinions as they need time to consider and reflect on any pronouncement they are expected to make. They can be extremely self-disciplined, sometimes austere and invariably, of all the types, they are the true aesthetes.

The Fingers

The shape of the fingers need not conform to the shape of the palm and it rarely follows that all the digits on one hand are all of the same kind; more often than not they are made up of a mixture of types. The fingers, then, should be analysed separately and added to the information furnished by the palm shape. It is by working on these separate levels, rather like a sculptor who slowly builds up the profile of a bust, that hand analysis suddenly comes to life and the picture of the individual emerges by degrees.

Square-tipped fingers

The square-shaped fingers (Figure 50a) follow closely the characteristics of the square palm and so each would complement the other. If, though, these fingers are seen on another type of palm they would add a

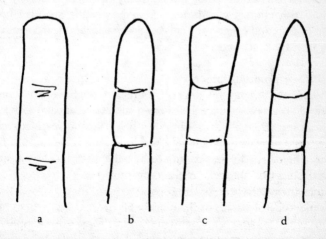

a   b   c   d

Figure 50

practical, pragmatic and earthy quality to the life. On a conic palm they would tame down the impatient and instinctive nature and bring a steadier approach to work. On the spatulate palm, square fingers would not present too much of a conflict but might just slow down the imaginative processes. On a psychic palm, square fingers might prove utterly disastrous as their plodding, materialistic and earthy manner would be in total conflict with the flights of fantasy and idealistic nature denoted by that palm shape. Happily, this combination is hardly ever seen.

Conic-tipped fingers

Conic fingers (Figure 50b) on a square palm would bring greater scope for adaptability and versatility to the otherwise stolid square. On the spatulate palm, this type of finger might aggravate the restlessness so that projects could be left hanging in mid-air whilst newer and fresher ideas are tried out elsewhere. This finger shape on the psychic palm could provide the necessary realism to turn the dreams and ideas into reality.

Spatulate-tipped fingers

These (Figure 50c) would add an inventive turn of mind to the square palm. On the conic, they could turn impatience into a more meticulously enquiring curiosity. But on the psychic, spatulate fingers might overtax and exhaust the delicate and fragile physical constitution portrayed by that shape.

Psychic, or pointed, fingers

On a square palm psychic fingers (Figure 50d) might set up a conflict but would certainly balance the earthy qualities of that palm with loftier spiritual and ethereal ideals. On both the conic and spatulate palms, these could provide inspirational ideas. Indeed, psychic fingers on any of the other shaped palms could produce the master artist, musician, craftsman, writer or great intellectual thinker of the day.

Apart from the shape of the tip of the digit, fingers may also vary in thickness, in breadth or in smoothness. The broader the fingers, the more self-assurance and self-confidence they portray. People with good, broad digits are often open-minded, tolerant, fair, generous and helpful. Very thin fingers can denote extreme austerity and may even suggest narrow-mindedness, cynicism and a mordantly critical mentality. Very smooth fingers show someone who is impressionable, possibly inspirational but whose ideas seem to come and go apparently without much processing. Knotted fingers, that is, digits where the joints are pronounced, denote the philosophical or analytical thinkers, those who like to take their time when making decisions and who generally love to chew over problems and issues in life.

Individual Phalanges

Each finger is made up of three phalanges, the top or nail phalanx, the middle one and the bottom one which adjoins the palm. The top phalanges represent the mental, spiritual and emotional expression of the particular finger. The middle one tells about the application or practical execution of the qualities described by the finger. And the bottom phalanx reveals the physical or material stance.

Normally, the bottom phalanx is slightly longer than the other two but, if the top and bottom ones are as long as each other, whilst the middle one is short, then this is the sign of the dreamer — someone who has good ideas but not necessarily the practical ability to bring them to fruition. In the cases where all the top phalanges are the longest then the individual will take a more intellectual outlook than a practical one in life. When the middle phalanges are the longest then it is in the managerial or practical abilities that the individual excels.

The next step is to take each finger in turn, to analyse its strengths and weaknesses and to see it in relation to its neighbours.

The index or Jupiter finger

The index represents the ego, the conscious self, leadership and responsibility. For the best indications, it should stand straight and be well-set on the palm in which case it shows a healthy ego with a goodly amount of self-esteem and self-respect together with a feeling of being in control of one's own destiny.

If it leans outwards, towards the thumb, it denotes a strong ambitious streak. The goals, aims and objectives of the ambition is dependent on the rest of the hand.

An over-long index, that is, one which is either as long as or even longer than the middle finger, denotes a need for power and control over others. On a good hand, this is the sign of an excellent leader of men. But, on a bad hand, one which shows weaknesses, misplaced aggression or vices, this formation can highlight the plain bully and the dictator.

A very short index, one which is considerably shorter than the ring finger, denotes a lack of self-confidence and a feeling of inadequacy. People with this feature prominent in their hands are often self-conscious and seem unable to control their own destinies. Moreover, if the finger is deeply set into the palm there could even exist a strong inferiority complex, the 'chip on the shoulder' type.

When the tip of this finger bends noticeably towards Saturn it tells of a person who likes to work quietly behind the scenes rather than in the full glare of the limelight. There is also a strong dislike of competition and anything of a cut-throat, rat-race nature should be avoided at all costs.

Long top phalanges here are often found on the hands of those involved in politics, religion and the law. Priests, prelates, military leaders, politicians, lawyers, judges or anyone in these professions worth their salt ought to have this particular feature on the index. Long middle phalanges, though, are to be expected on the executive types, those dealing in finance, business or industry. The long basal phalanges belong to trainers and managers in the sports world. If this phalanx is also full or broad it is often seen on the hands of those in the catering industries, chefs, restaurateurs or anyone who has a great appreciation of good food.

The middle or Saturn finger

This digit represents stability, security and the basic wherewithal for living.

If it towers over all the other fingers it can denote a 'Saturine' disposition, someone who is melancholy, down in the mouth, a bit of what we might call a wet blanket, possibly depressive and rather fixed in temperament.

A short middle finger, though, reveals the true Bohemian type, one who flouts the traditions, rules, customs and mores of the time. People with very short Saturn fingers especially loathe red-tape and petty bureaucracy.

A long top phalanx on this digit is often seen on the hands of researchers and particularly so amongst those who have an interest in any of the 'alternative' arts such as the occult, for instance. Long middle phalanges here have several interpretations. They may include the efficient housekeeper, adept at husbandry. Mathematicians, accountants, scientists or physicists may also possess this formation, as would farmers or all those who are interested in the land with the concept of conservation uppermost in their minds. Long basal phalanges would pinpoint the people who are extremely concerned with their physical and material stability. Historians might also have this formation. Short and podgy, though, this phalanx illustrates the greedy and the mean. But, when it is markedly narrow at the base, this is the sign of the eternal student — someone who is always interested in new ideas and in learning new subjects.

The ring or Apollo finger

This finger can represent one's creative and artistic disposition as well as the ability to express inner contentment and self-fulfilment.

If the ring finger is as long as, or even longer than the middle finger, this is the sure sign of the gambler, the over-confident speculator. This need not apply solely to punters, those who like to bet on the horses, for it may just as well apply to anyone who likes to take risks and chances in life.

If very short, this finger tells of a lacking in creative talent. Possibly someone who doesn't have an eye or any appreciation for the arts.

A long top phalanx shows an intellectual approach to art. A spatulate tip here is interesting as it is a sign of dramatic ability — actors and actresses invariably have this formation on their Apollo finger tip. Others who also possess this feature have a tendency to exaggeration: they are the ones who make mountains out of molehills, who blow up situations out of all proportions and who dramatize the least incident for histrionic effect. If the middle phalanx is long and lean it illustrates an eye for detail, line, colour and perspective. These are the people who are able to put their creative gifts into practice. A long basal phalanx shows good artistic taste but, if there is a fleshy bulge here, as seen in Figure 51, it is known as the 'collector's urge'. This can range from the highly selective and discriminating artistic eye of the antiques collector and dealer right down to the hoarder of brown paper and

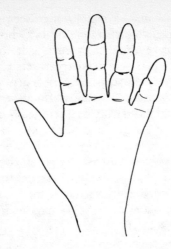

Figure 51

string! The difference between the collector and the hoarder is seen in the shape of the bulge itself: high and well-formed indicates the former, whereas full and shapeless denotes the latter.

The Mercury or little finger

This finger represents science and medicine as well as communication and the media. The general sense of self-expression is also illustrated by this digit.

A long, lean little finger is usually seen on anyone who is articulate, who is a good speaker or orator and who has a keen and ready wit. Literary types, writers, poets and those in the media often have this formation. A short finger, though, shows shyness, reticence and diffidence.

This finger should always be measured carefully because sometimes it may only appear short whereas in actuality it is fairly long but set rather low down into the palm. If this is the case then it is a mark of a profound lack of self-confidence.

A tip which bends towards the ring finger denotes the self-sacrificing spirit of the altruist. If the whole finger is bent, though, it has been said that this is the sign of someone who is dishonest and insincere. Usually, however, I have found this to denote an inherited physiological characteristic.

A long top phalanx on the Mercury finger is seen in the hand of the charmer, the person who has the 'gift of the gab', who can talk the hind legs off a donkey! Always expect a slick, silver tongue to go with this formation. Long middle phalanges here denote those in the caring or vocational professions — doctors and nurses for instance, although some scientists may possess this feature too. Finally, long basal phalanges on this Mercury finger may show a need for mental and physical freedom.

The Thumb

The thumb is the most important of all the digits as it is the key to the whole character and, as such, needs to be closely examined at this stage. It should, for best results, appear well-balanced and in good proportion to the rest of the hand. Sometimes, indeed, a thumb can look totally alien, as if it doesn't belong to the hand it's on at all and thus, instead of complementing and enhancing, it highlights conflicts and complexities. For example, a weak thumb on an otherwise strong hand would show a weakening of good potential and a lack of motivation with which to bring the aims and objectives to fruition. If the thumb is too strong for the rest, though, it would show an over-aggressive tendency to mask a weak character and poor personality traits.

The thumb represents will-power, motivation and driving force as well as the capacity for logic and reason. Like the fingers, it is made up of three phalanges: the top one reveals the individual's will-power; the middle one denotes logic and reasoning; and the basal phalanx is actually that part which is known as the mount of Venus.

Length
The length of the thumb should balance the palm and fingers and, in order to determine whether or not it does, a good rule is that the top phalanx should be longer than any single phalanx on any of the other fingers.

A markedly short thumb shows a lack of reasoning and logical powers. People with this feature tend to work instinctively and they may feel that they lack control over the events in their lives, that they are basically at the mercy of the prevailing circumstances. This is especially so if the thumb is both short and weak. But, if the whole thumb is not only short but also thick, so that it appears generally stubby, it illustrates quite a different sort of person, one who may lack sensitivity and even display signs of cruelty. Such people can crave power and so may become aggressive and ruthless in order to get what they want. In any position of power they can become despotic or tyrannical.

A long thumb denotes excellent rational powers. If it is not only long but aesthetically well-shaped too, it indicates elegance and refinement of thought and ideas.

The nail or top phalanx

This is the section of the thumb which represents will-power. The shorter the phalanx, obviously the less strength of will is implied. The longer, the more determination and will-power shown.

When this section is broad it shows someone who possesses the power of command, who tends to be the leader. This is the sort of person who can 'pitch in' with the rest without ever losing that presence of control or command. If the section is long but also lean this is again the sign of the leader but this time it's more representative of the theoretical or academic type of person. Those who have slender top phalanges here are able to get what they want in life with tremendous grace and charm. Full and padded, this section tells of an even temperament, an unflappable and steady sort of person.

A squared-off tip to the thumb conveys a practical, reliable and sensible disposition. A conic tip shows those who, although graceful in their approach, can easily become deflected from their goals and objectives in life. When this digit is spatulate in shape it is known as the 'potter's thumb' and, although it doesn't suggest that all those with this type of thumb should immediately buy themselves clay, turning-wheels and kilns, it does, nevertheless, highlight the craftsman, one who is manually skilled, sensitive and creative with his or her hands. If the top phalanx is pointed it can denote a nervous disposition, one who works in fits and starts.

The second phalanx

This is the section which deals with reason and logic. If it is very short in comparison to the top section then it tells that action will be instinctive and spontaneous rather than logically worked out. When it is of a good length it displays reasoned action. People with this formation admire articulacy, rhetoric and oratory. They are the ones who enjoy discussion and debate so much that they often sit up, burning the midnight oil well into the early hours, deep in argument over the topic of the day.

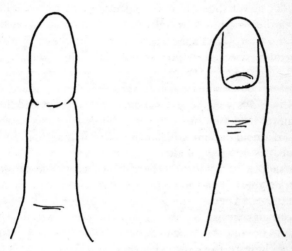

Figure 52   Figure 53

If, though, this phalanx happens to be longer than the top section (Figure 52), it reveals those who think more than they do. These are the people who over-rationalize; they analyse everything, working out all the pros and cons — so much so that they tire themselves out long before they are able to put any of their good ideas into action. This formation shows that there is too much logic and reasoning and not enough determination and persistence necessary to carry aims and objectives through to the end.

When, as in Figure 53, the second phalanx is 'waisted', that is, it narrows in the middle like an hour-glass, it denotes the tactician, the person who is always discreet and knows how to deal with others in a diplomatic fashion. Overly thick, though, and it tells of one who is blunt and to the point. A spade is a spade where these people are concerned, for they tend to see tact as simple evasiveness and eloquent language as a means of masking indecision.

Stiffness vs. Suppleness

Some thumbs are markedly stiff as there is no movement in the top joint, whilst others, the opposite of this, are supple and easily bend backwards at both top and bottom joints. Indeed, some are so extremely loose that they are known as double-jointed.

People with stiff thumbs have a tendency to inflexibility of character. They can be reserved, forceful types because they are very strong-willed and often 'play their cards close to their chests'. They are seen as 'closed' types because, with their self-control, they don't give anything away through emotional expression and so may appear as rather cold and clinical. Determined and persistent, they can withstand and resist hardships and it is this very doggedness which often leads to success in whatever field they are in. But their inflexibility can result in fixed ideas and a rigid outlook which can easily antagonize those who are somewhat more open-minded.

The supple thumb shows a flexible and adaptable nature. These people are able to bend and change and go along with the prevailing circumstances. They are the open, emotional types who hate to stick to routine and because of this can easily become distracted from their objectives. Because they tend to be open-minded they are able to reflect and quickly learn from their mistakes.

Those who have a thumb which is flexible only at the top joint may appear rather inconsistent — determined one day and distracted the next. That is because they are mentally agile and so like to jump from one activity to another.

When the thumb is double-jointed it may suggest a character weakness for such people seem to be all too easily swayed. They tend to give up or give in quickly for an easy life.

Setting and angle of opening

In my opinion, there is no satisfactory explanation, as yet, nor any real clarity in the literature on hand analysis which adequately distinguishes the differences between those with high-set as opposed to low-set thumbs. Personally, I have always found that the simplest explanation lies in the fact that the thumb which is set low down opens out wider and the one that is set higher up tends to form a tight angle to the palm.

When judging the angle of opening of the thumb it is important to remember the difference between how much a thumb can be stretched out and how it falls when the hand is placed comfortably on the paper. I usually take the former as a guide to the individual's potential but work more according to the latter, as this tells of the actual disposition of that individual at that particular time in his or her life.

Oriental tradition and philosophy says that the best angle is at 90 degrees for this shows total harmony of mind, body and spirit. Generally, however, I find that the norm lies somewhere between 45 and 90 degrees and this tells of an easy-going, optimistic, sunny character as illustrated by Figure 54 which is a print of a most charming and

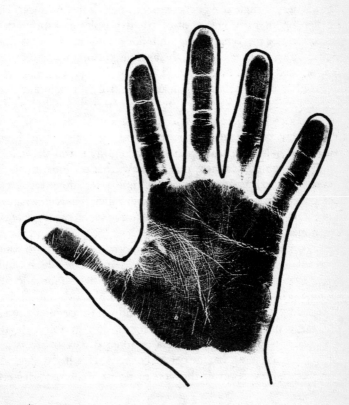

Figure 54

pleasant young lady. These people possess a healthy blend of both extroverted and introverted qualities so they are able to switch, quite comfortably, from deep concentration to an expansion of ideas.

If the thumb opens out to more than 90 degrees it tells of out-and-out extroversion. These people are characterized by extravagance in life, often self-indulgent and lacking in self-control. They have a great sense of adventure but, as they are unable to concentrate for any length of time, they can be distracted at the drop of a hat. Some may be quite uninhibited in what they do and say for they like freedom to express themselves openly in a non-conformist way. Because of this they can appear rather shocking at times to those who are a little more reserved in their attitudes.

A much tighter angle of 45 degrees or less reveals the introvert. This is the sign of intensity and control. Such people may suffer from repression and be martyrs to their inhibitions. They tend to have fixed ideas and opinions in life and, if the angle is very tight, they can be narrow-minded and even bigoted. It is often difficult to know what these people are really thinking for they are truly reserved and keep themselves to themselves. Very often, though, such a tight angle as this is a major clue to anxiety and to stress and tension.

Interestingly, people who are going through serious problems and worries often hold their thumbs stiffly and tightly at this angle. This seems to be a temporary measure and shows that the individuals are somehow reappraising their situations, mustering their resources, imposing greater self-control and concentrating their minds on whatever their problem might be, whether physiological, psychological, financial or emotional.

Picking up this kind of clue is of vital importance and so both hands must constantly be checked for any small discrepancies which would instantly throw a different light on attitude, behaviour and the development of a person's character. For example, a thumb may be held at a wider angle on the subjective hand whilst forming a much tighter angle on the objective one (Figure 55). In this case the discrepancy would highlight either a temporary state of stress and anxiety or it would show that the person concerned has had to conform and impose tighter control, through maturity, than was formerly necessary.

Conversely, if it is the thumb on the subjective hand which forms

Figure 55

a much tighter angle than on the corresponding objective one, then it would reveal that the individual had suffered a rather restrictive upbringing. This is sometimes indicative of early family problems or difficulties, possibly because of financial worries, possibly because of parental ill health or narrow attitudes or whatever. The wider angle on the objective hand, then, would indicate the opening out or the flowering of the individual through his or her maturity and independence.

CHAPTER FIVE

Finger Print Patterns

There can surely be very few people in our society today who haven't heard about finger prints. Devotees of Sherlock Holmes and detective fiction will readily tell us about the uniqueness of our individual prints, how no two patterns are alike, not even on the hands of identical twins. Taking a suspect's dabs has now become standard procedure and irrefutable evidence in law.

Unlike the other features in our hands, our prints do not change through our lifetimes but they grow with the individual through infancy to adulthood. Cut a finger tip, graze it, burn it or whatever and you will find that, with the healing process, exactly the same skin pattern returns. These are the patterns we are stuck with throughout our lives — our own personal and individual identification marks.

But these prints are not only to be found on our finger tips. In fact, the skin forms itself into patterns all over the palms of the hands and also the soles of the feet and these patterns are just as unique as the finger prints. On the hands, the skin markings are known as palmar patterns and, on the feet, they are called plantar patterns. The modern name for the study of skin patterning is *dermatoglyphics* which is derived from the two classical words: *derma,* which means skin, and *glyph,* which means a carving. So, literally, dermatoglyphics stands for the study of the skin carvings: those tiny ridges or furrows that form themselves into the familiar patterns we all know.

Origins

It was in the early nineteenth century when a Czechoslovakian physician called Dr Jan Evangelista Purkenje first identified skin patterns whilst working on the spiral sweat glands of the palm. This was the true beginning of the scientific study of what has now become known as dermatoglyphics.

Towards the end of that century, there was a British medical missionary in Japan called Dr Henry Faulds who, through his passion for archaeology, made a significant discovery in the field of dermatoglyphics. He found, when putting together many of the fragments of ancient pottery he had excavated, that a thumb print was pressed onto the base of the pots. He deduced, quite correctly, that these marks, then, were obviously used as the signature of the potter and that therefore the implication was that each individual's thumb print is unique.

This discovery was substantiated by a Commissioner of Police in India who observed that it was the custom for illiterate Indians to press their thumb prints onto official documents as their personal signatures.

Back in England, it was Francis Galton who, having heard of these discoveries, became the true pioneer of finger printing. Throughout his lifetime he collected and classified thousands of specimens and proved categorically the uniqueness and individuality of skin patterns. It was through his work that finger printing became universally accepted and used in criminal investigation and identification.

Today, modern hand analysts not only recognize the different patterns but, through observation and deduction, they have also attached character and personality traits to them. But it is in the medical field that a lot of exciting new research is currently being carried out in this area. This research is establishing a link between certain skin patterns and congenital or hereditary conditions, such as Down's Syndrome, and it is suggesting that these congenital malformations and chromosomal abnormalities somehow imprint themselves on the very skin patterns during the early stages of foetal development.

Finger Prints

There are three basic types of finger prints — the loop, the whorl and the arch — plus several other variations or configurations of these types. Some people have a complete set of one particular type of finger print but it's by no means uncommon to find an individual with a variety of these patterns on his or her hand. In such cases, each pattern must be interpreted according to which finger it is on.

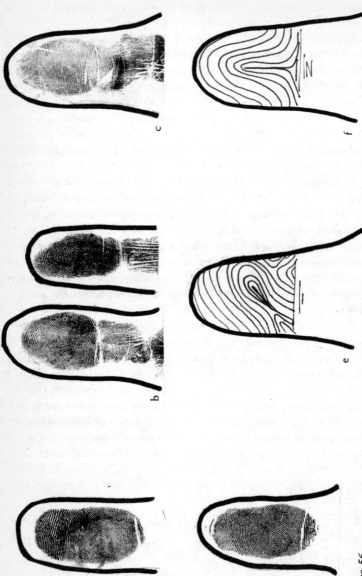

Figure 56

Loops

The most common finger print pattern is the loop (Figure 56a). Loops invariably indicate a need for variety and change. People with a full set of loops are generally flexible and adaptable. They love all sorts of new ideas and are at their best working with other people or in any situation requiring team spirit. Working in a rut or in a dead-end, boring, 9-to-5 job is anathema to them for they dislike routine and need to be constantly on the go and one step ahead. Indeed, these people thrive on challenge.

There are two forms of this pattern, the ulna and the radial loop. The ulna loop opens out towards the percussion side of the hand and is more commonly found than the other form. This type of loop shows that the individual is more readily adaptable and perhaps more easily influenced by others. The radial loop opens out the other way towards the thumb side and this is seen more on those who tend to take the initiative first although still remaining flexible and adaptable. This latter type is generally found mainly on the thumb and index but medical research is beginning to show that, if found on the third or fourth fingers, it could be one of the indicators of genetic defects.

A loop on any individual finger would indicate a flexible and free-and-easy attitude in whatever sphere of influence is represented by that digit.

Whorls

The whorl (Figure 56b) is a very individualistic sign and often denotes creativity. People with a full set of whorls are invariably seen as slow to respond; they need time to process information and formulate their ideas. Others may find these people infuriating or even frustrating and feel they want to shake some sort of reaction or response out of them. What compounds this situation is that they can be inflexible in their ideas and dogmatic in their views and they certainly like things done in their own way.

On the index, the whorl shows that, in a career or work context, these individuals prefer to be in charge and in control of their own particular jobs rather than have people constantly looking over their shoulders and telling them what to do.

On the ring finger, the whorl is an indicator of artistic or creative potential.

On the little finger, the whorl highlights the quiet and retiring types. These people are not idle chatterers but prefer to talk on matters they know and understand well. However, once they embark on their favourite subject it's almost impossible to stop them again!

On the thumb, the whorl especially denotes the slow types, those who are entrenched in their ideas and have particular difficulty in changing their views and opinions.

Arches

Arches (Figure 56c) indicate the practical, down-to-earth, salt-of-the-earth types. These people are reliable and trustworthy with an abundance of common sense. The problem with too many arches is that the individuals find it difficult to talk about their innermost feelings and their conversation more usually centres around concrete, everyday, material subjects.

Arches on the index and middle fingers especially highlight an inability to verbally express personal emotions and these people must find a practical outlet, such as painting, pottery, writing, etc., through which to express themselves; otherwise they could find themselves in danger of bottling up or repressing their feelings altogether.

On the thumbs, arches denote those whose feet are firmly planted on the ground and who are excellent at giving good, sound, practical advice. Because of this they often attract to themselves people with problems and tend to become valued as 'good shoulders to cry on'.

A full set of arches needs to be investigated thoroughly as this can, in some cases, indicate the possibility of chromosomal abnormalities.

Composites

The composite (Figure 56d) looks like two loops pulling in opposite directions, rather like the yin/yang symbol or the pattern on a tennis ball. People who possess this pattern have the ability to see both sides of an argument or the other chap's point of view. In decision-making or problem-solving, they tend to spend a long time weighing up the pros and cons, debating the advantages or disadvantages and working out the merits or otherwise of the situation at hand. Indeed, they may deliberate for so long that ultimately they either confuse themselves altogether or end up with so little energy that they are unable to take any concrete action. Because of their questioning or their need to know what's on the other side of the coin, they may sometimes be considered as argumentative, but more often this pattern stands for indecision and an inability to make up one's mind.

The composite is usually found only on the index and thumb and in these positions it bodes well for judges, lawyers, counsellors or anyone who needs to understand or appreciate the whole argument of any situation. But, at the same time, this can denote conflicting drives, confusion and difficulty in personal decision-making.

Tented arches
The tented arch (Figure 56e) is usually found only on the index. This has a similar meaning to the arch itself except that individuals sporting this pattern need some impetus or challenge behind them to fire their enthusiasm. Additionally, they may be single-minded or even obsessive types who feel compelled to be part of an ideology or a cause to motivate them in their everyday life.

Compounds
Sometimes an amalgamation of two different patterns may be seen on a finger tip such as, for example, a whorl inside a loop and this is known as a compound pattern (Figure 56f). When this occurs, it is important to decide which is the dominant pattern and then to interpret it accordingly. In the oriental tradition a whorl-loop is called the peacock's eye and when it is seen, especially on the third finger, it tells of a sense of protection to the subjects who find themselves in tight corners or in dangerous situations.

Palmar Patterns

Similar patterns to those on the finger tips may also occur on various other parts of the hand. Loops may be found on the palm between the fingers and the other patterns can occur on the mounts of Luna and Venus alike.

Between the thumb and index finger
In this position (Figure 57a) a loop generally denotes a courageous spirit.

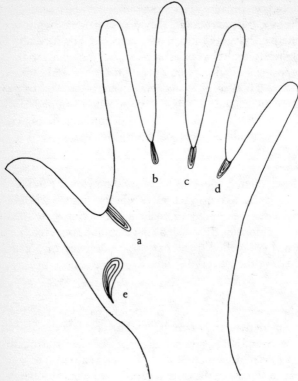

Figure 57

Between the index and second finger
Here (Figure 57b), a loop denotes executive ability and those possessing the pattern in this position are usually professional types.

Between the second and third fingers
When a loop is seen in this position (Figure 57c) it seems to indicate a rather serious intent in life. Invariably, these people have what is known as a vocational spirit and they have a fundamental need to work for the community or for the good of others.

Between the third and fourth fingers
This is the sign of a rather dry and odd sense of humour (Figure 57d).

The mount of Venus

Most markings on this area (Figure 57e) suggest musical talents of one sort or another and, if the owners of such markings don't actually play a musical instrument, then great musical appreciation at least is indicated.

The mount of Luna

This is an area which can be rich in skin markings, and loops, whorls and composites may all be found here.

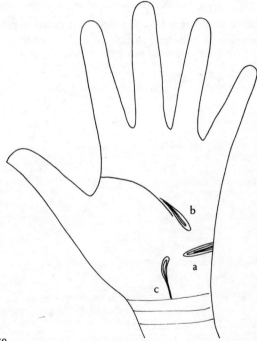

Figure 58

1. A loop lying across this mount (Figure 58a) denotes a love of nature, an understanding of, and a rapport with, flora and fauna.
2. A loop following the head line downwards into this area (Figure 58b) may suggest a good memory and excellent powers of retention. I have found that in most cases when I have encountered this

particular pattern it reveals an affinity to water. There is invariably some kind of connection with rivers or the sea either in terms of location or sporting interests or, simply, that the subject feels drawn to water and is enormously invigorated by it.

3.   A loop rising upwards from the wrist (Figure 58c) is the mark of inspiration — that delicate and ethereal stuff that poets and painters are blessed with.

4.   A whorl in this area often suggests a special gift or talent. Sometimes, those who possess this marking feel a great longing to fulfil themselves either creatively or through commitment and service to humanity.

5.   A composite pattern here would indicate personal uncertainty or indecision regarding the individual's gifts and talents.

PART TWO

The Lines

CHAPTER SIX

The Major Lines

When considering any line on the hand it is important to distinguish between its direction and course as opposed to its structure and composition. The former lays down our basic characteristics whilst the latter tells about our psychological and physiological state. Any anomalies on the lines, such as branches, cross-bars, breaks, etc., highlight particular events in our lives.

The lines are formed in the embryo some time, it is believed, between the second and third months of foetal development and it is fascinating to see just how clear these lines can be on the hand of a new-born infant. It must be remembered that lines can, and do, change throughout our lives according to our experiences, decisions, changes of life-style, states of health or whatever events occur to us which modify our awareness of ourselves and our environment. This is of vital importance as it confirms that we are not 'stuck with our fate' but that, in fact, we have free will to choose and make our own 'destinies' for ourselves.

The other factor to be borne in mind here is that the hand is an excellent indicator of potential and possible future events. Because of this, a good analysis of the lines can not only provide insight into personality traits, but can also shed light upon the likely outcomes of our actions and decisions; and by thus alerting us well in advance this can enable us to prepare ourselves for any eventuality or alternatively take any necessary steps to obviate those events from happening at all.

There are four major lines on the hand, as illustrated in Figure 59, which are the head, life, heart and fate lines, together with several other major lines besides. Some hands may have so many lines that they seem almost to be covered by a fine cobweb whilst other hands have only the three or four main ones. The hand that is covered in lines

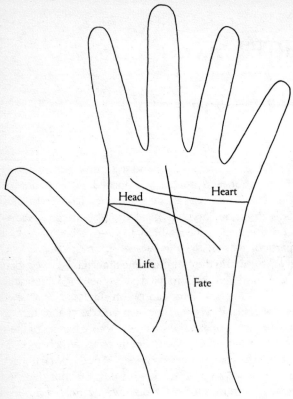

Figure 59

is known as the 'full hand' (Figure 60) and this reveals a sensitive individual, someone who is perhaps rather highly strung and who has a tendency to worry. Such people have delicate nervous systems whereas, those with the few lines, known as the 'empty hand', seem to be steady, robust types and virtually untroubled by their nervous systems. These people, it may be said, are usually less sensitive and less nervous than those bearing the full hand.

The actual quality of any line is something which must be immediately taken into account and it is important to note which line stands out from the rest, whether because of its strength or its weakness, as this will act as the keystone to the whole interpretation of the lines.

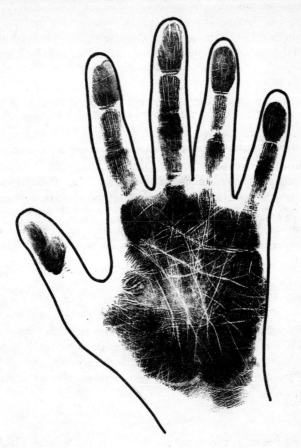

Figure 60

When considering the structure of the lines there are a few rules which help the general assessment:

1. Deep, fine lines = positive, cohesive, channelled, clear-cut.
2. Wide and on the surface = pliable, amenable, easily distracted.
3. Islanded/chained = worry and/or possible mineral/chemical imbalances.
4. Broken = change of awareness or life-style, or possible injuries.

Always remember when studying the lines that the information they give must be superimposed on whatever has already been learnt from the rest of the hand — from the shape, the fingers, the skin markings or whatever. In this way a complete picture is built up with each level adding, confirming, corroborating and refining the concepts revealed in the whole hand.

Another point to remember is to check any discrepancies in the lines between the right and left hand as these will highlight any differences or conflicts between how individuals may view themselves, how they feel instinctively and how they behave in private as opposed to the picture they may put across of themselves in public, how they have matured and how others may see them. On right-handed individuals, it is the right hand which represents the persona, the adult, the public side and it is known as the objective hand. The left, then, represents the anima, the inner feelings, the private and domestic side and so is known as the subjective hand. On left-handed individuals, of course, the principles are reversed.

The Head Line

I believe this is the most important of all the lines as it represents our intellectual potential, our mental stance and outlook on life. A good, strong head line indicates that the subject has the power to overcome most other physical, psychological or emotional problems that may be seen elsewhere on the hand.

Position
The head line begins at the palm edge just above the thumb. It is the second transverse line as it occurs below the heart line and lies across the palm.

Strength
The strength of the line must be gauged according to all the other lines in the hand.

A clear, untrammelled, unbroken and well-etched line would be considered a strong head line (Figure 61a). People with such a line as this would be rather strong-minded, positive, forthright individuals

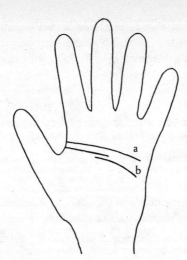

Figure 61

who find making decisions comparatively easy. They are clear-sighted, intellectually independent, decisive and generally possess clarity of mind.

A faint, broken (Figure 61b), chained or islanded (Figure 62a) line would be viewed as a weak head line. Owners of this sort of line could

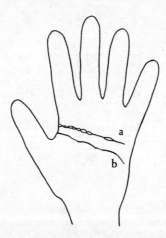

Figure 62

be typified as indecisive and would find decision-making particularly difficult. Perhaps they might be plagued with worry and anxiety of one sort or another and they might, at times, lack concentration and clarity of thought.

It is quite possible that a line could be strong in places and then weaker in others, as shown in Figure 62b. Such a formation would obviously show periods when the subject is sharp and mentally alert and then, through pressures, for example, times of possible indecision and 'cotton-wool' thinking.

Direction

If the head line lies straight across the palm, as in Figure 63a, it indicates a practical, pragmatic mentality and a convergent thinker. These people have a fairly materialistic outlook and they normally take a rational, concrete, down-to-earth approach to life. If they are academically minded then they would favour the scientific subjects. Business and commerce, too, would suit them and anything of a technological nature.

The line which curves gently downwards (Figure 63b) reveals the more creative or artistically minded person, the divergent thinker. Such folk are found in the humanities; anything connected with communications, languages, design, arts and crafts in general and dealing with other people would suit those with a curved head line.

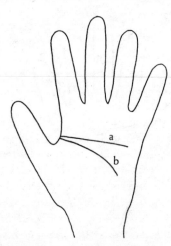

Figure 63

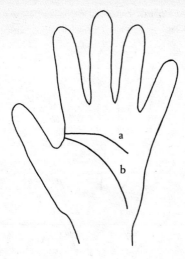

Figure 64

When the head line travels in a straight course towards the centre of the palm and then starts to curve downwards (Figure 64a), it shows a combination of the practical and creative mentality. These are the people who can equally enjoy the arts as well as the sciences and, because of this, they find it difficult to choose which they prefer. The best advice in these cases is for them to think about the more applied subjects, the softer sciences or anything which combines practicality with creative flair. If they are in a scientific or an out-and-out practical job then they should try to cultivate some creative hobbies. Alternatively, those who find themselves in purely artistic occupations ought to think about a more concrete and practical pastime with which to balance out their interests.

A steeply curved line ending low down on the mount of Luna (Figure 64b) reveals tremendous imagination which, if unrestrained, can lead to melancholia and depression. In extreme cases, these people can be so imaginative and so creative that, it may be said, they could teeter on that brink of genius and madness. Certainly, these are the types whose moods can easily swing up or down and so may be considered as manic depressive. Generally, they tend to work in spurts — greatly enthusiastic one minute and fed up the next. The best advice for these people is for them to try to harness their energy and to channel their moods into creative output because only in this way will they allow their rich imagination and artistic talents to develop and flower.

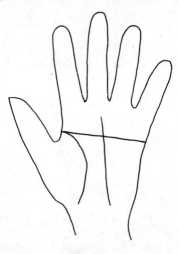

Figure 65

There is a fairly unusual feature which does occur and which is called the Simian line (Figure 65). This line is formed when the two lines of head and heart are fused together into one single line lying right across the palm from edge to edge. Although the Simian line is one of the most recognizable signs of Down's Syndrome it does occur in about 6 per cent of normal hands. In the normal hand, this line is the mark of intensity. People with a Simian line have the ability to concentrate, to channel their thinking, for they can be very single-minded. In a sense, they tend to compartmentalize every facet of their lives so that, when they are concentrating on their work, they can only think about that job. When they concentrate on a hobby they totally switch off all else and focus solely on that. It's almost as if they can pull the shutters down so that they can devote and dedicate themselves to whatever it is they are engaged in at that moment in time. Emotionally, too, this intensity can manifest itself in jealousy; for, as they give themselves totally to the ones they love, so, too, they expect their love to be reciprocated to the exclusion of all others and of all else. If the Simian line, rather than being one single line, has the tails of the heart and head lines projecting from it, as seen in the

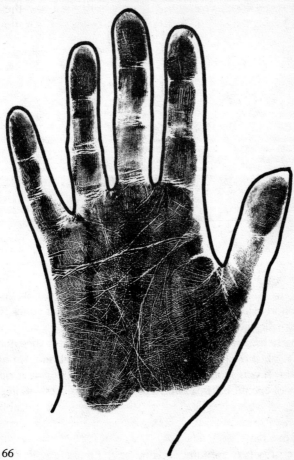

Figure 66

example in Figure 66, then the intensity is eased and the jealousy mellows with growing age and experience.

Length

I believe that the actual length of the head line can give some important insight into the scope and intellectual potential of the individual.

A short head line, that is, one that ends under the middle finger (Figure 67a), reveals a somewhat earthy and mundane mentality. Those

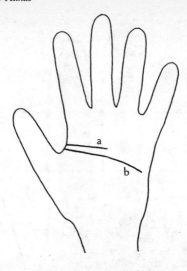

Figure 67

who possess such a line seem to be more concerned with material security than others and their conversations, more often than not, run along concrete lines. For example, rather than abstract concepts, they prefer to talk about cars, holidays, houses, clothes, money, etc.

A long head line, one which runs past the base of the ring finger (Figure 67b), shows a keen intelligence and an aptitude for abstract thought — just as long as, of course, the construction of it is sound. This sort of line promises excellent prospects for successful intellectual abilities.

The course
The next step is to minutely scrutinize the line along its course, as this will, quite staggeringly, bring to light much psychological detail and insight into the character of the individual and the events surrounding his or her life.

Beginnings
When the head line begins attached to the life line, as seen in Figure 68a, it reveals a cautious, careful nature. Often, this can also show a closeness to the parental influences and early environment. If the lines are united for a considerable distance, not separating until under the

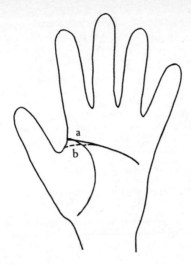

Figure 68

middle finger, it tells that the subject is a late developer, probably not becoming truly independent until much later than most.

If the head line actually begins inside the life line, as shown in Figure 68b, it points to someone who is insecure, self-conscious and possibly even lacking in self-confidence. As a consequence, this type may become aggressively defensive through life.

A good blend of caution and impulsiveness is seen in the hand where the two lines detach themselves quite early on or where a small gap is seen between the two (Figure 69a). This is also a mark of self-confidence.

When the two lines are markedly separated then the individual is the adventurous, reckless and impulsive type. People with this formation are extremely independent and show it at a very early age. Invariably they are dare-devils and the young girls will be tomboys. 'Live now, pay later' seems to be the axiom that fits these hands.

The higher up the palm the commencement of the head line, the more ambitious the nature. These people are the cerebral types, highly achievement-motivated with plenty of drive to attain their goals and expectations in life. Generally, they don't let their emotions interfere with their rational processes for, with them, it's very much a case of their 'heads ruling their hearts'.

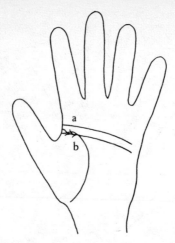

Figure 69

If, at the beginning, the line appears intricately interwoven or intermeshed with the life line (Figure 69b), or if it is islanded or chained, then either of two interpretations could apply here. Firstly, the health of these people may not have been all that it should throughout their youth or, alternatively, they experienced early worries and anxieties, often not feeling quite in harmony with their parental or childhood environment. Other factors in the hand should help to distinguish which of the two alternatives apply.

The point of separation
Do examine this point carefully as it reveals the process of maturation and how the individual actually achieves independence.

If the attached head line lifts itself up and away from the life line quite close to the edge of the palm (Figure 70a), then it can be said that such individuals almost bodily lift themselves out from their early environments, almost as if by their boot-straps. One way this could happen might be through academic achievements, for example.

When islands or crossing bars are present at the very point of separation (Figure 70b) then it would appear that independence came with considerable emotional upsets. Possibly interference or opposition may have been placed in the way of the individual's desire for independence and freedom.

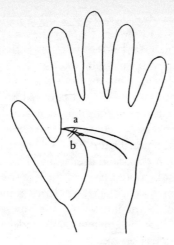

Figure 70

If the two lines separate cleanly and neatly, then the transition from childhood to independent maturity occurs easily, harmoniously and with no major upheavals.

The first half of the head line
As the line travels beneath the index finger it represents the early years of life from birth to about twenty (Figure 71). So it is in this first section

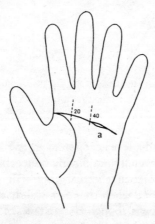

Figure 71

of the line that the developmental years, the parental influences, the educational progress and, finally, the maturation process is seen. As I have already shown, any islands during this period denote worries, emotional upsets or possibly ill health through this time. Any branches seen rising up to the index mount from this point usually indicate academic achievements or feelings of personal success.

The next stage of the line, travelling beneath the middle finger, represents the early twenties right through to about forty (Figure 71). Again, islands on this section (Figure 71a) would highlight worries which last for the duration of the island itself. Any change in the structure or composition must be noted. Should the line strengthen, then the thinking processes improve with greater clarity of thought and a more positive outlook. But, if the line weakens in any way then it would be fair to say that lack of concentration, indecision and general intellectual weakness has set in.

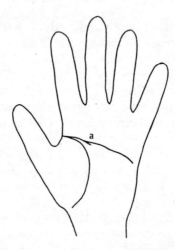

Figure 72

Sometimes, the head line may appear to zig-zag up and down (Figure 72). This formation, even if only slightly noticeable, represents peaks and troughs in the subject's intellectual progress through life. The peaks indicate periods of time when thinking is clear and channelled and unhampered. The troughs, though, denote times of possible depression, when intellectually the individual is at a low ebb.

Any dip in the line or downward pointing branch, no matter how tiny, as illustrated in Figure 72a, will highlight times of 'low', when the subject is experiencing emotional problems and feels generally depressed.

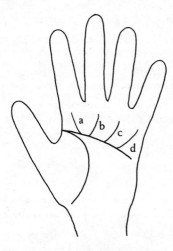

Figure 73

Conversely, any rising branch represents mental achievement. Rising branches towards the index finger usually indicate academic success (Figure 73a); towards the Saturn finger (Figure 73b) may show career prospects and achievements; towards the ring finger (Figure 73c) highlight feelings of creative fulfilment and satisfaction; towards the little finger (Figure 73d) show either scientific or business success or possibly even financial gain.

A break with overlapping ends along any part of this line is most interesting for it represents a complete change of awareness, a reorientation, often a completely new way of looking at life. People with this feature seem, because of experiences of one kind or another, to undergo a whole process of change. Through this time they question their ideas, their long-held beliefs; they challenge their values and reassess their objectives and ideals. In this way they emerge with a totally different outlook on life and this is seen according to the position and quality of the new section of line.

If the new overlapping line lies above the old one, thus closer to

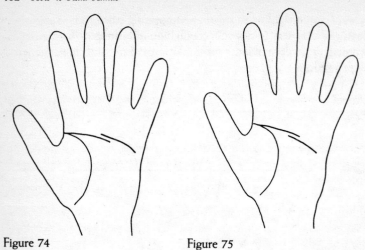

Figure 74   Figure 75

the heart line (Figure 74), the individual emerges more practically minded, more business-conscious, possibly a little harder but much more in control than before. If the new section commences underneath the old one (Figure 75), then the individual becomes more relaxed, more expansive and perhaps much more open and creative than ever before.

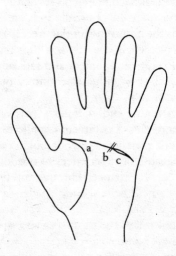

Figure 76

A clean break, with no overlapping ends (Figure 76a), is an unusual feature and could possibly denote an injury to the head or a remarkable event which would end one part of the individual's life quite dramatically before opening up another.

Crossbars at any point cutting the main line (Figure 76b) represent times of interference, opposition or setbacks which temporarily impede the natural flow and hamper the progress of the individual. If, after the obstruction, the line continues as normal, then the interference has no long-lasting detrimental effects. Any damage from such events would be represented by islands (Figure 76c) or a weakening of the line itself.

The second half of the head line
As the head line travels across the palm below the Apollo finger it represents roughly from forty onwards. If the line is short it does not in any way infer a short life, but simply that the time scale should be compressed. Some hand analysts maintain that dating on this line is perhaps not recommended but I have found my method quite satisfactory and invariably successful.

The same rules should be applied to this part of the line as those of the first half. Note the structure here too, whether any changes, either of a positive or negative nature, occur. Are there any noticeable islands, bars or breaks here which would suggest worry, opposition, interference or change? If downward branches are seen, these, as in the previous section, would indicate periods of depression. Rising branches, though, denote times of achievement. On this section it is quite unusual to see branches shooting off to the index or middle finger mounts, but, if they do exist, they would be interpreted as academic and career successes. More usually, if there are rising branches, they would point towards the ring and little fingers. Towards the ring finger suggests personal and creative fulfilment and satisfaction; to the little finger, would denote scientific, commercial, technological or financial achievement.

Endings
If the line thins out towards the end it shows that there is more potential there but the mind is not being stretched to the full. The stronger the line at its termination, the more vigorous and alert the mind becomes with growing age.

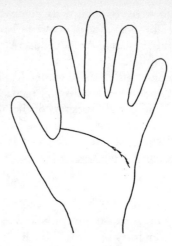

Figure 77

When a line is tassled, split or frayed at the end (Figure 77) it can denote forgetfulness in old age and a general dissipation of mental energy. This can be one of the signs of senility.

In some cases the head line splits itself into a fork but this must not be confused with the fate line which rises up and cuts through the line. When the line forks under the middle finger (Figure 78) it may

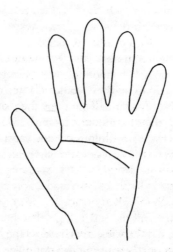

Figure 78

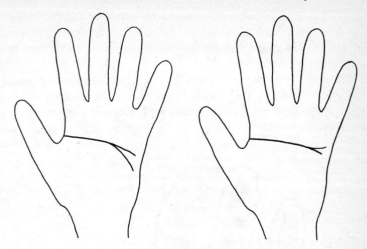

Figure 79   Figure 80

denote a talent for music or alternatively an aptitude for anything to do with property and the land. Forking beneath the ring finger (Figure 79) is rather special and is known as the 'writer's fork'. Not all writers have this mark nor indeed do all who possess it become writers. What it does show, though, is excellent creative or artistic talent. If the line forks below the little finger (Figure 80) it highlights business, commercial or financial expertise.

Discrepancies between the right and left head lines

Hand analysis becomes a fascinating study when differences are detected between the two hands as this reveals richness of character and complexities in the individual. Remember that, on a right-handed person, the right hand portrays the objective side whereas the left illustrates the subjective and, of course, vice versa for a left-hander.

Should the objective hand display a stronger head line than the other, whether it be in terms of length or structure or composition, then it can be said that such individuals have made more of their intellectual development than their inherited or early environmental background would have allowed.

If, on the contrary, it is the subjective hand which bears the stronger line, then the owners of this feature have not made the most of their intellectual capacity nor of the opportunities presented to them in life. Should the head line be forked at any point on the subjective hand alone it would suggest that potential for expansion in those areas has not yet been developed.

Notice the differences between the two head lines in the prints of the right-handed lady illustrated in Figure 81. The left head line is much longer and sweeps down considerably further than the right one. This would show an intrinsically imaginative and artistic mind but one which

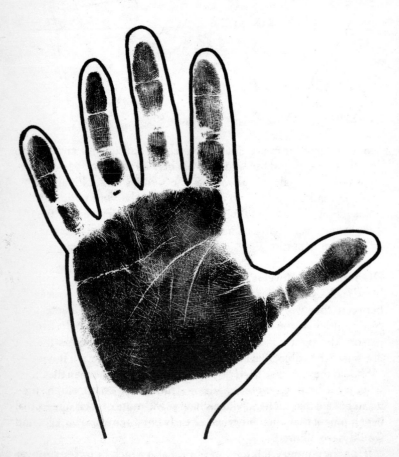

Figure 81a

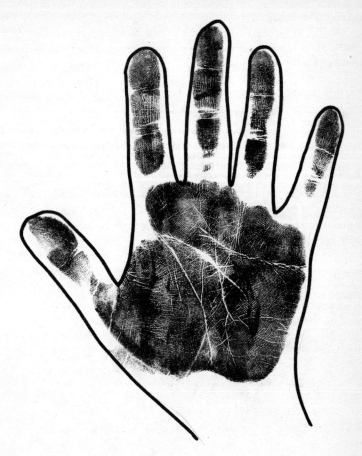

Figure 81b

is tempered and kept in touch with everyday reality by the more pragmatic line on the right. Overtly, she is coolly rational whilst maintaining a strong creative streak and thus the two lines, when taken together, present a balanced outlook of creativity and pragmatism. When not in harmony, however, she could be in danger of allowing her rampant imagination to turn into bouts of pure fantasy.

It is by minutely studying any discrepancy in this way that the art of hand analysis really brings the subject to life.

The Life Line

The life line represents our vitality, our enthusiasm for living, our zest or verve for life. It can reveal our state of health, whether we are strong and robust or weak and frail and generally it reflects the actual tenor of our lives. The fundamental mistake that so many people make with regard to this line is that they believe it reveals the actual length of the life itself. Indeed, this is a fallacy and it must always be remembered that the life line represents the quality *not* the quantity of life.

Position

The life line is found beginning at the palm edge, usually half-way between the base of the index and the thumb. From its commencement it may then form a wide sweep into the centre of the palm or it can skirt tightly around the thumb.

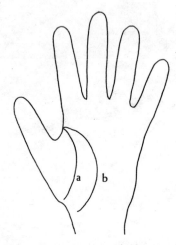

Figure 82

When the line is seen to hug the mount of Venus, keeping close to the thumb (Figure 82a), it illustrates a lack of vital energy and a general lack of physical robustness. People with this formation may be, what is known as, rather sickly types. Alternatively, they tend to show emotional coolness and a certain personal reserve.

The further the line sweeps towards the centre of the palm (Figure

82b), the stronger and more robust the constitution. These people are generally virile and active, with plenty of stamina and vitality. They have a great enthusiasm for living life to the full and they seem to simply exude human warmth and charisma.

Beginnings
The indications revealed by the beginning of the life line follow exactly the same principles as those described on the head line. If the two lines begin attached, this denotes a cautious, self-restrained individual and, if the lines remain attached for a long way, then it is the sign of the late developer. When the lines are attached but separate early on, or indeed, when there is a slight gap between the two, there is a good balance of common sense and caution together with a spirited sense of fun and adventure. A wide gap between the two indicates impetuosity, someone who enjoys taking risks and chances in life, the adventurous, dare-devil type who tends to leap in at the deep end before working out all the consequences.

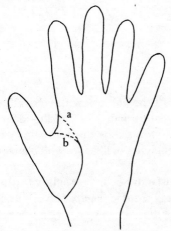

Figure 83

The average starting point of this line is roughly half-way down the palm from the base of the index finger to the thumb. The higher up the line commences (Figure 83a) the more ambitious and possibly, even masterful the individual. Beginning lower down towards the thumb (Figure 83b) reveals uncertainty and a lack of self-confidence.

Islands

Wherever an island is seen on the life line it reveals a weakening of the constitution, a period of ill health or simply a general lacking of robustness lasting for as long as the island is present.

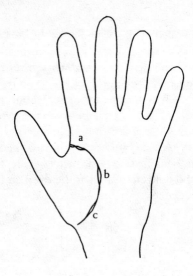

Figure 84

At the beginning of the line below the index finger, an island, or indeed a chain of islands, indicates childhood or early adolescent illnesses (Figure 84a). Invariably, this formation here represents the bronchial or catarrhal types of illnesses which affect the nose, throat, chest or sinuses.

I have found that islands occurring slightly further down along the line often denote back trouble (Figure 84b). This could simply infer a general weakness of the back or spine or, in some cases, actual injury to the back itself.

Still further down the line towards the wrist, an island would indicate any weakness or ill health mainly associated with growing old (Figure 84c).

Islands must be investigated in conjunction with the other features in the hand in order to establish physiological weaknesses and to ascertain the exact nature of the illness implied.

Breaks

There are two types of breaks which may be seen on this line — a complete, clean break and one where the lines overlap.

In the first case, a clean break can denote an accident or the possibility of sudden ill health. If a square formation is seen over the break itself (Figure 85a) it marks some form of protection against the danger, a cushioning effect which acts as a buffer to the events and so bodes well for a speedy recovery.

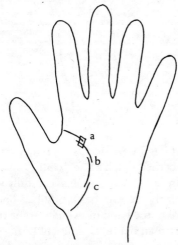

Figure 85

When a break is seen with the ends of the lines overlapping, it indicates the development of a brand new section of life line and, as such, represents a change in the life-style, new beginnings, new horizons or a change of environment. The wider the space between the overlap, the greater the change. If the new section of line begins inside the old one (Figure 85b), then it would show that the changes bring a narrowing, a cramping, of the new life-style as opposed to the old one. This might occur, for example, after an accident where the individual's health has weakened or, perhaps, after an unhappy move. But, if the new section begins outside the old, that is, towards the centre of the palm (Figure 85c), then the new life brings great improvement, wider horizons, more activity and a general feeling of expansion.

A word of caution here. Sometimes a life line is seen which appears

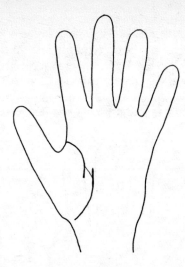

Figure 86

to be unusually short (Figure 86) and as such may give great anxiety to the individual concerned. Such a line, it must be stressed, does not indicate a short life. In fact, if it is examined carefully it will invariably become apparent that this feature has a tiny hair-line joining it to a new line in the centre of the hand or even, in some instances, to the fate line itself. Rather than denoting an early death, then, this type of line, in fact, reveals a brand new life altogether at the time indicated — possibly these people might emigrate, for example, or marry or move into quite a different world to the one they had previously been used to.

Branches
There are two types of branches which come off the life line: those which rise up towards the fingers and those which drop down towards the wrist.

Rising branches are also known as effort lines for they stand for personal triumphs, a sense of accomplishment, of having succeeded over the odds. Up towards the index mount (Figure 87a), a branch would suggest academic endeavours. Towards the middle finger (Figure 87b) would imply successes connected with property, with domestic stability or with occupational matters. A branch which rises towards

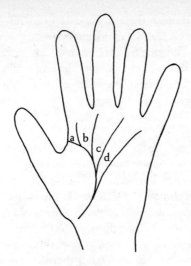

Figure 87

the ring finger (Figure 87c) highlights creative fulfilment and contentment. One rising towards the little finger (Figure 87d) reveals a sense of satisfaction in anything connected with scientific, literary, commercial or financial affairs.

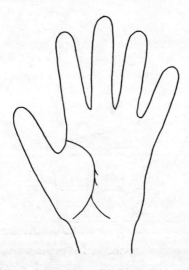

Figure 88

Branches which drop downwards (Figure 88) denote movement, either implying a change of address or journeys and travel in general. The tinier the branch, the smaller the move as, for instance, moving to a new house. But the longer the branch, the more important the move. A long branch often represents travels abroad, especially so if the branch penetrates deep into the Luna mount.

Crossing lines

Lines which lie across the life line are called trauma lines and indicate times of obstruction, opposition or interference all of which create great emotional upheaval or turmoil. The bolder the crossing line, the bigger the upset. If the cross bar begins at the base of the thumb and travels over the main line, this suggests problems of a family or parental nature. If the cross bar cuts right through the life line and then proceeds to cut through the head and/or heart line, this is the sign of a really big emotional upheaval (Figure 89a). If there are many of these lines but they are fine and closely packed (Figure 89b) they show, rather than specific events, that the individual is perhaps highly strung, fretful and prone to worry. When a cross bar begins from an influence line (see below) inside the main life (Figure 89c) line it tells that the problem stems from that relationship.

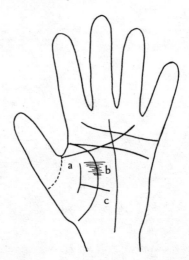

Figure 89

Influence lines

These lines are seen on the inside of the life line, either springing out from the line itself or independently paralleling it. Those which spring from the body of the line itself (Figure 90a) may, in most cases, denote children. The independent lines (Figure 90b) stand for relationships and friendships and the quality of these lines will reveal what sort of influence the relationships have upon the individual.

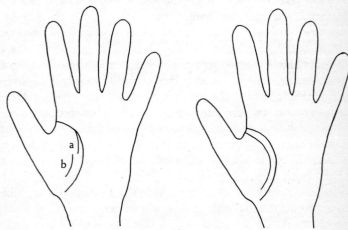

Figure 90   Figure 91

Sister lines

A sister line is a parallel line which follows the life line on the inside throughout its length (Figure 91). This is also called the line of Mars and it has two interpretations. Firstly, this feature can represent a strong influence such as a close and loving soul-mate or sometimes, even, a rich inner spiritual life. In other cases, this line suggests extra vitality and protection, rather like back-up reserves, especially so if the main life line is broken, chained or islanded, where it seems to add a boost to the vital strength and life energy.

The Heart Line

The heart line relays information about our emotions, our attitudes to love, marriage and relationships. Interestingly, this line can also hint at health matters, particularly about the heart itself and about our general body chemistry and mineral imbalances. There are two schools of thought regarding the beginning of this line. The traditional approach is to interpret the heart line as commencing somewhere beneath the first two fingers. Some of the modernists, however, maintain that the line should be analysed from the percussion edge first and then up towards the fingers. Although I can appreciate both points of view, I prefer to take the traditional approach on this point and so I shall stick to this interpretation here.

Position

The heart line is the first transverse lying across the palm directly beneath the fingers. If it appears to lie considerably high up in the hand, so that it seems to be very close to the fingers (Figure 92a), it reveals an intellectual approach to the emotions. These people are cool, rational, analytical, the sort whose head rules the heart.

Lower down on the palm, so that it is displaced closer to the head line (Figure 92b), shows that the emotions take precedence, that, in fact, the heart rules the head.

If the line is very straight, especially if this formation is seen on a female's hand, it usually denotes a shrewd and sometimes even a

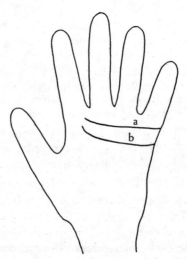

Figure 92

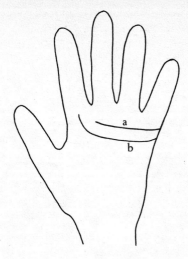

Figure 93

calculative approach to human relationships (Figure 93a). The straight heart line has often been referred to as a 'masculine' heart line.

Alternatively, when the line is deeply curved (Figure 93b) it highlights a generous, giving and sensitive approach to relationships. Whether this is seen on the male or female hand it is referred to as a 'feminine' line. Whenever it is seen, this feature also indicates a strong sense of justice, of mercy and of fair play — so strong, in fact, that people with this type of line invariably go to great pains in order to give others chance after chance to redeem or to explain themselves, often ending up getting kicked in the teeth for their trouble.

Beginnings
The line which begins on the index mount (Figure 94a) indicates idealism in affairs of the heart. These people tend to have a rosy picture of relationships and marriage, seeing their lovers rather like knights in shining armour or fair damsels in distress. These are the people who have extremely high ideals and even higher standards of excellence. As a consequence, they are in danger of suffering disappointments and disillusionment when they discover that those they have placed on a pedestal are merely human and that, like everyone else, they too have feet of clay. When they are let down in this way, it takes them

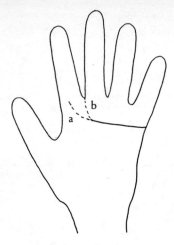

Figure 94

a long time to regain the love and trust they had invested — if indeed they ever do. The best advice here would be that they should try to lower their expectations, to be more realistic about relationships and about human nature in general.

If the line begins very high up on the index mount, almost reaching the base of the finger, it can indicate jealousy and possessiveness not only of lovers and husbands but of children and friends too.

When the line is seen to begin between the first and second fingers (Figure 94b) it shows a sensible, down-to-earth attitude to marital relationships. These people are warm-hearted and, because they find it difficult to express their inner feelings verbally, they prefer to show their love through action. This can, though, lead them to bottling up their emotions, both negative and positive, and may end up repressing them altogether. In this case they need a safety-valve, either a good ear to listen to their problems or perhaps a diary or journal in which to pour out their feelings and thus release them. Ideally, they ought to try to verbalize their inner emotions, to express their feelings in words, as this not only clears up misunderstandings but also gives others the sort of confirmation they need.

A line which begins under the middle finger (Figure 95a) denotes sensuality and, it is said, these people have a tendency to view relationships as purely vehicles for sex.

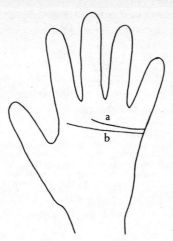

Figure 95

For people who have a line which travels straight across the palm (Figure 95b) beneath the index and beginning almost at the palm edge, it is work which comes first every time because their jobs and careers are extremely important to them. All other aspects of life have to fit in accordingly and their loved ones have to learn to give them the necessary space and time they need to pursue their work. These are

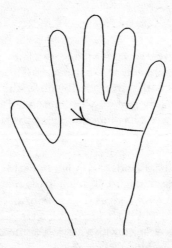

Figure 96

the people who, because of the devotion and dedication to their work, are often found on committees, or called upon time and time again to shoulder responsibility.

A line which has three forks (Figure 96) is considered to be the ideal as it encompasses all the categories described above — the warmth, the idealism, the passion and the sensible approach to all human relationships and dealings with others.

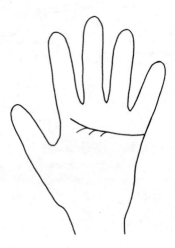

Figure 97

Branches
Branches which drop downwards off the heart line can represent times of emotional disappointments and unhappiness (Figure 97). The deeper and longer the branch, the stronger, obviously, the upset. Any rising branches, although fairly rare, may be interpreted according to their direction in the same way as those applying to the head line.

Islands
When seen on the line, islands may point to health disorders. Under the index/middle fingers (Figure 98a), an island may indicate hearing difficulties. Under the ring finger (Figure 98b) an island could show potential sight defects whilst a laddering effect here may also pinpoint nervousness, edginess coupled with a possible disturbance in the normal sleep pattern, perhaps due to a lack of calcium. In general, a chained

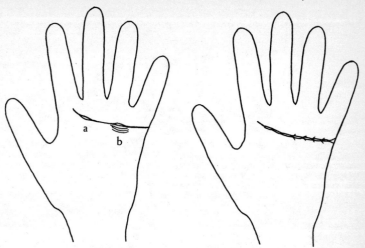

Figure 98   Figure 99

heart line may be indicative of mineral deficiencies or imbalances (Figure 99).

Any other markings on this line, such as breaks or dots, could be potential pointers to certain cardiac or vascular conditions but these must be verified by other indications or factors elsewhere in the hand.

The Fate Line

The fate line represents our public selves, our careers, our way of life and the general awareness of ourselves, our roles and our standing in the world.

Beginnings
This line can have several starting points but the normal rule is that the fate line rises up the hand, usually through the centre of the palm, and travels towards the fingers.

If it takes its roots from the Luna mount (Figure 100a) then it reveals a career which needs to be connected with other people, being in the public eye or, better still, in the limelight. People with this line need public approval and approbation.

Those who have a fate line which begins attached to the life line

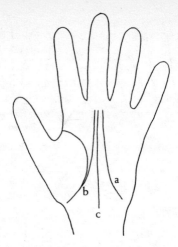

Figure 100

(Figure 100b) invariably experience early family responsibilities and commitments. A boy who takes over as head of the family due to the loss of the father, or a young daughter who feels it her duty to care for her sick parents, might both have the fate line attached to the life line. It is not until the lines separate that the responsibilities change and the individuals feel free to pursue their own independent lives.

When the line travels in a straight course right up the middle of the palm (Figure 100c) it highlights those who, in a sense, pre-plan their lives or somehow follow a set pattern which, to others, might be considered a bit of a rut. Due to such factors as increased mobility and the unemployment situation, this sort of line is not seen quite as often these days as it used to be for it represents a certain predisposed path in life, such as might be seen on those who follow in their father's footsteps, or who are employed in the same firm from the time they leave school until they retire. In addition, the line in this form also adds a touch of fatalism to the individual's philosophy of life.

The fate line may begin higher up on the palm but it is not until it starts that it marks the beginning of a sense of control over the environment, the idea of responsibility and the feeling of purpose and commitment in life. In a few cases, the development of this line may indicate feelings of restriction or entrapment but this would, of course, have to be analysed according to the rest of the hand.

The course of the line

If the line is faint or fragmented, especially so at the beginning (Figure 101), it denotes vacillation, no firm ideas about the future, perhaps a lack of purpose or direction and it also shows frequent changes of jobs.

Where the actual texture of the line is uneven, sometimes appearing thicker and then thinner, it tells of varying degrees of control the individuals feel they have over their lives — sometimes they may feel in command and then, at other times, they may feel at the mercy of their environment or of the prevailing circumstances.

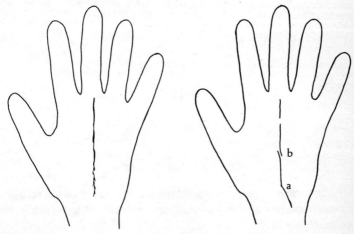

Figure 101   Figure 102

Any breaks, or even the slightest deviations in the line represent changes in the life-style or modifications in occupational or career matters (Figure 102a). Where there is an overlap (Figure 102b), the new branch indicates the beginning of the new life or new job, generally a new direction in life. Usually, if the lines overlap it denotes a smooth transition from the old to the new life, often initiated by the subjects themselves. A clean break (Figure 102c), however, suggests a more sudden termination of the old life, more often than not instigated by others, as in the case of a redundancy, for instance. The new life, then, is taken up with renewed vigour when the next section of line appears. It is the size of the gap or deviation in the line that marks the sort of difference from one phase of the life to the other. A slight kink here would suggest a small change such as a promotion or a side-step within the same company. Alternatively, a very wide space between the two sections of line implies a completely new start, a total change of career, a new environment and a different life-style altogether.

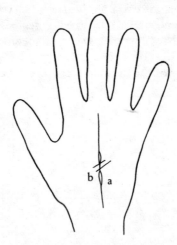

Figure 103

Islands in the line itself (Figure 103a) show periods of worry, possible disillusionment or frustration at work or at home or, in some instances, financial difficulties.

Any bars seen cutting across the line (Figure 103b) reveal set-backs, interference or opposition to the normal course of events.

Branches
Branches which rise towards the fate line from the area of the mount of Luna denote influences or relationships in the subject's life. Should the branch actually meet and join into the main line itself (Figure 104a), this is interpreted as the consolidation of the relationship, usually marriage. Whether that relationship has a positive or negative effect on the individual can be judged by the appearance of the fate line immediately after the merger. If the line continues strong and straight then the relationship has a good effect. If, however, the line forms an island, or is interrupted by cuts or bars, it would be considered that the relationship brings with it certain difficulties. If the fate line breaks

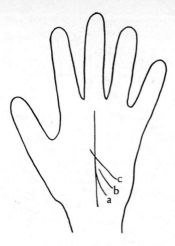

Figure 104

after the union and then is recommenced by a new section, then the relationship would bring changes, either a change of location or, it would mark the beginning of a whole new way of life.

It has been shown that if an influence line from Luna fails to join into the fate line (Figure 104b) or, if it cuts right through the main line (Figure 104c), then this bodes ill for that relationship. Both these instances suggest that the relationship either won't last long at all, or, it is likely to have a detrimental or disastrous effect on the subject.

Branches rising from the fate line and reaching up towards the index mount (Figure 105a) are fairly uncommon but might show some form of public recognition. As that part of the hand represents anything connected with politics, the Church, the law and even education, a branch in this direction could imply success in any of those areas depending on the individual's career.

The normal ending of the fate line is below the middle finger so it would seem most unlikely to find a branch rising up there.

Rising towards the ring finger (Figure 105b), any branch would highlight artistic or creative achievement and, possibly even, success. Certainly, this branch indicates a feeling of satisfaction in the progress of the subject's career or way of life. Make sure not to confuse a branch in this area with the Apollo line which can sometimes spring from the body of the fate line itself.

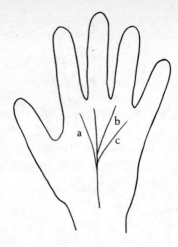

Figure 105

A branch seen to rise towards the little finger (Figure 105c) implies some form of success connected with science, commerce, business or financial affairs, again depending on the individual's career.

Parallel lines

If a branch is seen rising from the Luna mount and, instead of meeting the fate line runs alongside it (Figure 106a), thus forming a parallel line

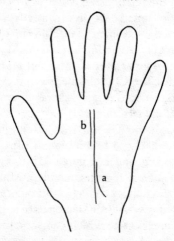

Figure 106

to it, then this is one of the best signs of an excellent partnership, usually indicating a good marriage where the two individuals feel like partners rather than husband and wife.

Elsewhere along the course of the fate line, a parallel line has two interpretations (Figure 106b). It can either mean a double career, as in the case of someone who maintains two part-time jobs, say. Or, it can imply a duality of roles as in the example of a person who has a normal daytime career but is also, for example, a local politician, in his or her spare time. One thing is for sure, this type of double fate line invariably indicates increased activity.

Endings

The normal ending for this line is on the mount of Saturn, below the middle finger although it may terminate elsewhere on the hand.

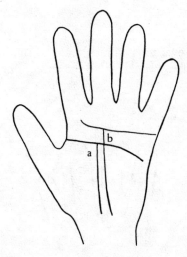

Figure 107

If the line should suddenly stop on the head line (Figure 107a) and does not resume at all then it is quite possible that an occupational misjudgement or a wrong move has seriously damaged the career.

Ending suddenly on the heart line (Figure 107b) might suggest that an emotional entanglement or setback (sometimes even a major scandal) has had a detrimental, if not even a catastrophic, effect on the career.

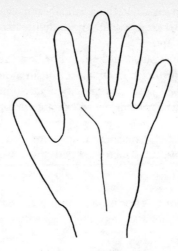

Figure 108

If the line swings over to end on the index mount (Figure 108), it is possible that the subject could indeed end up somehow in the public eye — if not becoming famous in itself, at least attaining some sort of public acclaim or recognition.

Figure 109

If the ending sweeps over into the Apollo mount (Figure 109), beneath the ring finger, then a career totally bound up with creativity or art would be implied.

CHAPTER SEVEN

The Minor Lines

The Sun Line

The Sun line is also known as the line of Apollo (Figure 110a). It may not be present in all hands but when it is it shows personal contentment

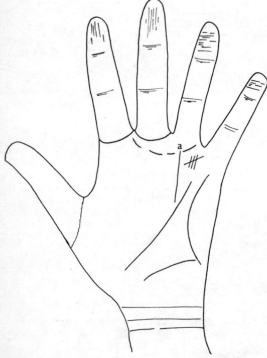

Figure 110

and satisfaction with the way our lives are going. Creative fulfilment and a feeling of success usually accompany the presence of the Sun line. It has been said that those with a strong Apollo line are talented and gifted people and, although this may be true amongst a great proportion of them, I have found that it implies, rather, a certain fundamental happiness with life and a time when peace of mind is attained.

The Sun line works together with the fate line for they seem to back each other up. Should one show weaknesses, in terms of breaks or islands, then the strength of the other would compensate for it. A good, strong line of Sun would denote a person who is well-endowed with Apollonian characteristics, that is, outgoing, cheerful, creatively talented; someone who is easy to befriend and who makes friends easily because of a warm and sunny disposition.

Beginnings
This line may rise from several points. If it is seen starting from the base of the palm near the wrist (Figure 111a) it is a fairly rare sign of early success, such as a young gifted actor or pop idol might possess, for example.

When the line springs from inside the life line, that is from the Venus

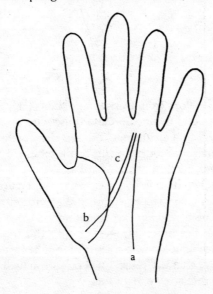

Figure 111

mount (Figure 111b), and shoots out to the Apollo mount, it denotes that the family has been responsible for contributing to the success of the individual.

If the line rises like a branch from the life line itself (Figure 111c) and then makes its way to the Apollo mount, then it is through the individual's own achievements that success is attained.

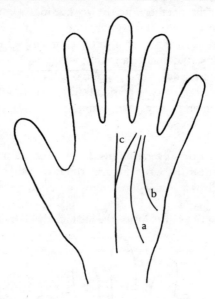

Figure 112

When the line develops from the mount of Luna (Figure 112a), this is often a sign of public recognition and those who possess it often achieve their success either in the media or somehow in the public eye.

If the line commences a little higher up, on the mount of Mars (Figure 112b), success is achieved only after hard work.

Springing from the fate line and then rising up (Figure 112c), this Apollo line suggests an enhancement of the career itself and adds to the individual's general feelings of contentment and satisfaction.

Beginning above the heart line (Figure 113), this line suggests a comfortable old age coupled with a sense of well-being and peace of mind. It also implies that the subject will be surrounded by warmth and love through the latter part of life.

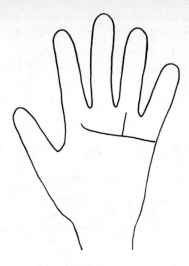

Figure 113

Absence of the line
Sometimes the sun line may not be present at all in a hand and although this does not show a complete lack of success, nor indeed abject failure, it does, nevertheless, show that life may not be quite as smooth or as easy as it might and that success, if achieved, comes with struggle and hard work.

Plurality of lines
People who have several sun lines running side by side (Figure 114) are the sort who tend to have many interests and, because of this, may not make a success of any at all. 'Jack of all trades and master of none' might be an appropriate epithet for these people or, alternatively, it could be said that they have too many eggs in one basket. If they are the sort of people who like to have an active, buzzing life with masses of things to do, then many sun lines would indeed be most suitable for them. But this does suggest, though, a scattering of energies over a large area rather than a concentration of effort on a single goal.

Traditionally, three sun lines rising above the heart line (Figure 115) is a sign of luck when it comes to money and financial affairs. For these people money seems to turn up, even at the last minute, just when they need it most. They may never, in fact, be millionaires but at least

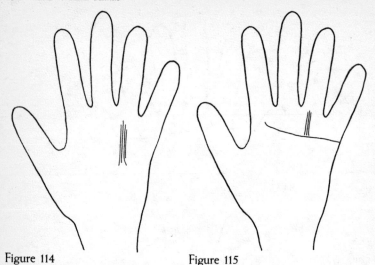

Figure 114   Figure 115

they can be confident that they will never be totally without. Whether it is that these people have a knack in handling their money matters, or whether they are just 'born lucky', is a debatable point. The plain fact of the matter is that, when they need it, the money seems, like magic, to appear.

The Mercury Line

This line (Figure 116) has many other names for it may be known as the health line, the business line or the hepatica. It is a complex line to interpret mainly because not enough satisfactory research has, as yet, been carried out on it.

The line itself can be seen rising from anywhere around the base of the hand, more often than not from the Venus or life line area, and then rises to end on the Mercury mount under the little finger.

It may seem strange to combine the idea of health with business indications in this line but it does suggest information, according to the type of hand, on whether the health of the individual is likely to upset his or her sense of business. The concept of *mens sana in corpore sano* is appropriate here, that is to say, that clear-headedness due to

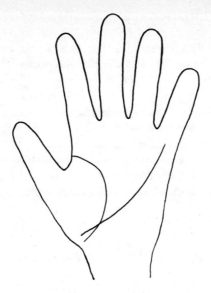

Figure 116

a healthy constitution leads to sharp and quick decision-making in any business dealings.

The very presence of this line on the hand does not, as has been thought in the past, mean bad health. It can, though, mean that these subjects are aware of their own health and perhaps have a sensitive nervous system. It is interesting to note, however, that a poor Mercury line, one that is islanded or frayed or twisted, can, in fact, denote a sensitive constitution and a lack of physical robustness.

It has also been thought in the past that the point at which the Mercury line cuts the life line means certain death at that time. This is quite erroneous and such nonsense simply spreads fear and alarm. It is possible that such an indication may suggest ill health, or a weakening of the constitution, but this must be judged according to its strength in comparison to the other lines, coupled with the fact that other health factors in the hand must also be taken into consideration here.

In my mind, the explanations surrounding this line are not at all satisfactory and much work has yet to be carried out in order to investigate it thoroughly and clear up its many ambiguities.

The Bow of Intuition

The bow of intuition (Figure 117) appears as a semi-circular line on the percussion edge of the hand. People who possess this line are, as the name states, highly intuitive and perspicacious. They are incisive, with keen penetrating insight, which means they can clearly judge a situation or read someone like a book. They have, in fact, what is often called a sixth sense for they can often 'feel' what is going to happen in the future even if they can't rationally explain it. The stronger and more complete the line, the more sensitively perceptive they are. Such people also have vivid, lucid and colourful dreams which, especially in times of trouble, may have more than a touch of precognition in them.

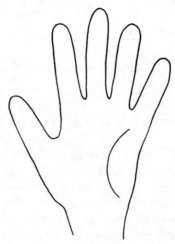

Figure 117

If this formation is seen on the subjective hand alone, then the owner has inherited this gift but has not developed it to its true potential. Those who have the line in a clear and strong formation on both hands should always rely on their instincts and be guided by their inner feelings as these won't lead them far off the mark.

The Girdle of Venus

This line is a bow formation (Figure 118) which may be seen under

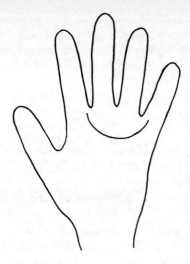

Figure 118

the base of the fingers and above the heart line. Some say that when present it denotes sensuality but I believe that it, in fact, indicates creative ability through heightened sensitivity.

If the formation exists as a complete semi-circular line and if there

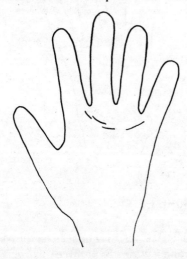

Figure 119

are also other signs of weakness in the hand, then the extreme sensitivity implied may turn to suspicion or even paranoia. But, if the line is broken or fragmented (Figure 119) then it shows that a good deal of common sense tempers that sensitivity and the individual becomes receptive and sympathetic to others.

The Via Lascivia

This is another line which, like the Girdle of Venus, has been much maligned in its time (Figure 120). The modern interpretation for the Via Lascivia is that it can reveal sensitive physical reactions to various substances, and people who possess this line should take care with chemicals, alcohol, tobacco, drugs or their general diet. Because they may be allergic to any of these, they should also be aware that the presence of the line can equally indicate a potential for addiction. The Via Lascivia is also known as the allergy or poison line.

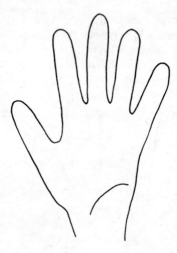

Figure 120

The Medical Stigmata

The Medical Stigmata (Figure 121) may be seen on the Mercury mount below the little finger and it is formed of three small vertical lines with

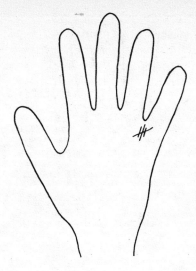

Figure 121

one crossing it horizontally so that it looks a little like a television aerial. When seen it denotes the special gift of healing. Not all those in the medical profession have this mark, nor indeed do all those who do, go into medicine. Many who possess it simply have a soothing, compassionate nature which surrounds them and spreads to those with whom they come into contact, often emanating an aura of calm and serenity around themselves. Others use it actively, if not as doctors, nurses or vets, in counselling roles or generally helping those in need. Yet others still, find that they are able to 'sooth a furrowed brow', or bring active relief to those in pain, and particularly so to young children, simply by running their hands over them. Certainly, this is a special and wonderful gift and those who possess it should do all they can to develop it and use it for the benefit of mankind.

The Ring of Solomon

The Ring of Solomon (Figure 122a) is a small semi-circular formation around the base of the index finger. When seen it shows that experience and the lessons learnt in life have brought wisdom and understanding to the subject.

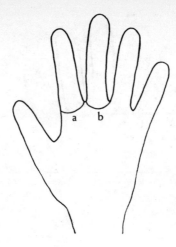

Figure 122

The Ring of Saturn

This is a semi-circular formation and, if found, is seen around the base of the middle finger (Figure 122b). A fairly uncommon marking this, usually existing for only a temporary period whilst the subjects fight against a sense of frustration, a feeling that their footsteps are dogged no matter what they do. Much as they try, they feel that they are being dragged back so that their endeavours amount to very little in their minds. If this attitude persists for a long time, these people can end up rather bitter and extremely cynical about life.

Sympathy Lines

These are a series of oblique lines (Figure 123a) on the mount of Jupiter below the index finger. This formation highlights someone who has great understanding of people and of life and who displays qualities of sympathy, empathy and human warmth.

Lines on the Finger Tips

Lines may occur on the finger tips, both in a horizontal and vertical

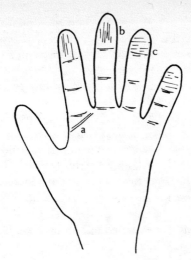

Figure 123

position, from time to time (Figures 123b and c). Horizontal lines are usually temporary features and are a sign of stress and tension. The accurate interpretation of these lines can be extremely beneficial to the subject as they can pinpoint and explain the very source of the problems and disquiet being experienced at the time. It is by simply establishing on which finger, or fingers, the greater concentration of lines occur, that it is possible to tell the nature of the problem.

Lots of horizontal lines on the index tip would suggest worry concerning the subject's ego or standing in life, maybe even professional or occupational problems. On the middle finger, lines show anxieties regarding one's sense of security, property or home. On the ring finger, the lines would hint at personal unhappiness, a sense of unfulfilment and general dissatisfaction. Many horizontal lines on the little finger tip indicate worries concerning one's abilities of self-expression. Occasionally, lines here might also point to problems in the individual's sexual relationships.

These lines do disappear as the problems and worries are resolved but what is so fascinating about them is that it is even possible to tell at what stage the problems have reached. What happens is this: the lines on the objective hand change more rapidly than on its counterpart so, when a right-hander, let's say, begins to worry about a problem, horizontal lines will start to form on the appropriate finger tips on the right hand. As the problem progresses and sets in, the lines subsequently become evident on the left finger tips too. When the anxieties are resolved and the problem sorted out, the lines on the right hand clear away first, leaving those on the left to fade away in due course.

If, therefore, more lines are seen on the finger tips of a right-hander's objective hand then it can be said that the problems are only just beginning but, if there are more on the subjective hand, then it would be fair to say that the worries are nearly over.

Vertical lines on the finger tips are quite a different matter altogether. It is possible that these formations may indicate hormonal imbalances depending on which of the finger tips the lines are mostly concentrated. More research needs to be carried out in this area, however, before any really conclusive evidence can be given.

The Family Ring

This line (Figure 124a) is seen curving round the base of the thumb. Any trauma line stemming from this line, travelling across the Venus

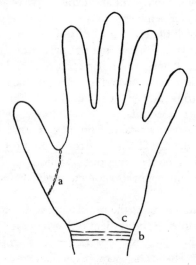

Figure 124

or Mars mounts and cutting the life line, would indicate problems directly connected with one's parents, relatives or close family ties.

The Rascettes

The rascettes, or bracelets, as they are more commonly known, are seen on the wrist just below the palm (Figure 124b). It used to be thought that the more rascettes seen, the longer the individual's lifespan was likely to be. This, in my mind, doesn't seem to bear any weight at all although this feature can be useful when considering the individual's health. If the top rascette on the wrist bows upwards into the palm itself it may indicate internal delicacy and particularly gynaecological complications in women or urological problems in men (Figure 124c).

Islands, Bars, Squares and Stars

Whenever an island is seen in a line it tells of some form of weakening or problems connected with the area represented by that line. On the head line (Figure 125a), for instance, it would suggest worry whilst on the life line (Figure 125b) it may indicate illness or a weakening of physical robustness.

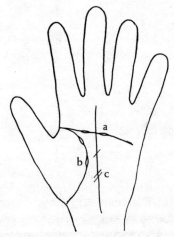

Figure 125

A bar across a line (Figure 125c) is usually indicative of a temporary barrier, either in the form of opposition, obstruction or some kind of interference in the normal course of events. The nature of the problem is often highlighted by other factors seen elsewhere on the hand and occurring at the same time.

Squares are known as protective marks for they denote that circumstances surrounding the individual somehow act as a buffer or cushion any unpleasant events or occurrences illustrated on the hand. For example, a square surrounding a break in the life line would suggest some form of protection against, perhaps, accident or danger. If a square is seen, not over the fate line, however, but attached to it as illustrated in Figure 126a, it tells of a period of hard work, a time when these individuals may feel plagued with frustration and limitation. If, though, they use this time well by getting down to some hard, constructive work and thereby consolidating their efforts, they should find that they are laying down the foundations for their future, smoothing the path for the years to come.

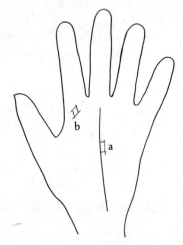

Figure 126

Another square with a different interpretation is the teacher's square (Figure 126b). This formation may be seen on the Jupiter mount below the index finger and, when present, it reveals a natural ability to impart information to others. Not all those who possess this mark become teachers, by any means, nor indeed do all teachers have it in their hands but, those who do, have a wonderful way about them, especially with children, and I often regard them as the Mary Poppins of this world.

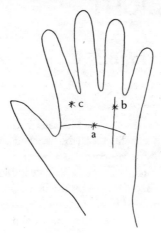

Figure 127

Stars may be seen actually on the lines or alternatively they may stand independently in any area of the hand. The general rule is that a star on the line may represent a shock, an unexpected event whereas, independently on a mount, it can denote success. So, if a star occurs on the head line, for instance, as seen in Figure 127a, it may show a time of mental crisis — a sudden major worry maybe, or perhaps, even, a mental breakdown. On the fate line it could indicate a sudden unexpected or possibly alarming event. On the life line it might suggest an accident. The only exception to this rule, I have discovered, is that a star on the Sun line doesn't so much denote a shock but rather a surprise, and one, more often than not, that brings some kind of acclaim to the individual (Figure 127b).

Standing proud on the mounts, then, the star denotes success in whatever field is represented by that area of the hand and it must, therefore be interpreted accordingly. On the Jupiter mount, however, is an exceptionally lucky spot to have this formation as it illustrates a general, overall potential to succeed in life (Figure 127c).

CHAPTER EIGHT

Time on Our Hands

Unlike astrology where, if the exact details of birth are obtained, the timing of events in our lives can be worked out with stunning accuracy, in hand analysis the precise timing of events is not so satisfactory. Certainly it is highly possible to establish the likelihood of particular events and occurrences on the hand within a certain time span, sometimes even refined to an extremely narrow period of time, but it is still not possible to predict to the very month let alone the actual day.

Nevertheless, the ability to assess whether something is likely to happen to us within the next few months as opposed to the next few years has its obvious merits and it is preferable by far to not having any clues at all. The advantages of knowing the possible trends our futures will show at least allows us time to plan our lives and to make contingencies within that time. The beauty of timing events on the hand is that we can see for ourselves, in graphic detail, whether it is that a line grows stronger or develops islands, bars, branches, changes direction or whatever it might be, before our very eyes.

There are various schools of thought as to the method of assessing and timing events. This is because hands do not come in uniform sizes so any scale or gauge that is used has to be tailored for each individual. Accuracy, though, does come fairly quickly after some practice but it is wise, at the beginning, to establish a particular event, say an emotional upset, accident or achievement, which would be strongly marked and then to work out the rest of the timing from there. In fact, even after years of experience, I still prefer to confirm times and dates with a subject first, especially so if the hand is unusually larger or smaller than average, before going on to make a prediction. The reason for this is because, to my mind, my skills are not there to be 'tested' but to be used in order to help, to guide or to furnish a better understanding of the person who seeks my knowledge.

The lines which are used for the purpose of dating and timing are the life and fate lines. However, I also use the head line quite satisfactorily for timing events despite the fact that some say it is not too reliable a source. Finally, it is much better to work from a print because accurate measurements can be taken with a ruler rather than trying to make any assessments from the actual hand itself.

Time on the Life Line

Time is read on this line beginning from the radial edge, below the

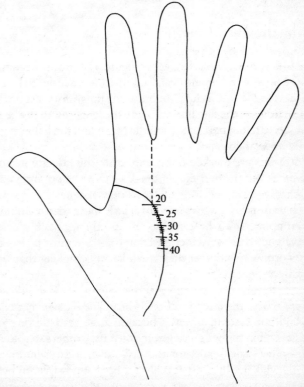

Figure 128

index finger, around the thumb and down towards the wrist. In general, I find that roughly a millimetre represents the span of a year but care must be taken to compress or expand the scale according to the size of the hand. A good rule of thumb is to establish the 20th year and work forwards and backwards from that point and, as illustrated in Figure 128, there is a quick method for setting this mark.

Draw a line straight down the inside edge of the index finger and where it meets the life line is roughly 20 years of age. From then on each millimetre can be marked off and, incidentally, after a while the measurements become so automatic that a ruler is not needed at all. Another good tip is to mark off 25, 30, 35, 40, etc. with a longer dash than the intermediate years so that these can be picked out at a glance when analysing the events on the line.

Time on the Fate Line

The fate line is read, as illustrated in Figure 129, from the wrist up towards the fingers and timing events on this line is a little trickier than working on the life line as it is not quite so straightforward. In order to establish time on the fate line, measure the length of the palm from the top rascette to the base of the middle finger and the half-way point represents 35 years of age.

Now, 35 years are marked out evenly from the rascette up to this mid-way point but, from there on the scale must be compressed lest we assume that every person's life span only reaches 70! Below 35, then, each year may be represented by a little more than a millimetre, above that point by a whole millimetre and then, possibly past the 50s, by even a little less. Remember that the scale must be modified further according to whether the hand is larger or smaller than would be normally expected.

There are those who maintain that the 35-year mark should be set at the point where the fate line cuts the head line. I have my personal doubts about this system, however, because some head lines are found lying considerably higher up or lower down than others so that there seems to be no logical basis for this type of measurement.

Again, as with the life line, it is always best, if possible, to find an

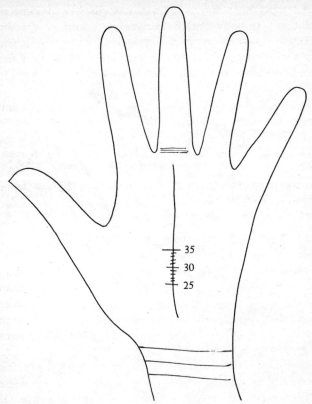

Figure 129

event which is strongly marked on this line and confirm its timing with the individual concerned and then work around that.

Time on the Head Line

Timing events on this line is comparatively easy to do (see Figure 130). The 'millimetre a year' rule applies here and, as on the life line, the 20th year is established by drawing a line down from the inside of the index finger to touch the head line. The age of 35 is also established, this time by drawing a line down from the centre of the middle finger to meet the head line. Yearly intervals can then be marked off accordingly using these two marks as reference points.

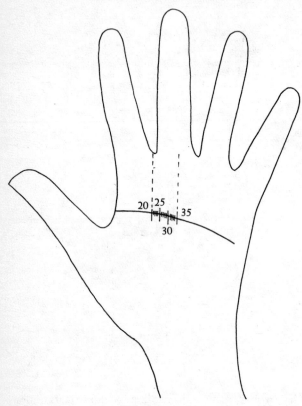

Figure 130

PART THREE

Applied Hand Analysis

CHAPTER NINE

Relationships

When it comes to the question of relationships there are many factors in the hand which must be taken into consideration. Firstly, there is the nature of the relationship itself, whether it is that of brothers and sisters, business associates or perhaps a romantic attachment. Different clues lie in different areas of the hand according to the type of relationship in question and these are built up, layer by layer, until a full picture of the situation is revealed.

Level 1: Hand Type Compatibility

In all cases, compatibility of types must be established first and foremost, so the first factor to look at when making this sort of comparison is the actual shape of the palm. Check for palm shapes in Chapter 4, 'Working from a Print' before embarking on this exercise.

It is the shape of the hand which lays down the basic character of the individual and so those with similar shapes will have the same fundamental disposition. There are, though, various shapes which really would not get on at all well together and yet others still which, if put together, would certainly let the sparks fly! To gauge the basic compatibility of types, first establish the shape of hands of each individual and then check them off on the list below.

Square with square. Two square hands are compatible and would represent a solid, united, practical and sensible pair of people.

Square with conic. The conic is infinitely adaptable and versatile so it is possible that these two could strike up a common basis for a workable relationship. They may, though, be in danger of frustrating and annoying each other as the routine, plodding ways of the square could bog down the conic type with his or her need for change and variety. Similarly, the conic's impulsiveness could quite throw the more methodical and concrete nature of the squared hand.

Square with spatulate. These two would certainly get on in terms of energy levels alone. They are both constantly on the go, active, busy beavers and, although the spatulate might have more creative imagination, the square would provide the practical application.

Square with psychic. These two would be quite disastrous together. The earthiness of the square would completely stultify the ethereal qualities of the psychic whilst the psychic's vagaries would jar at the logic and realism of the square.

Conic with conic. Both compatible together, each would stimulate and excite the other.

Conic with spatulate. Also compatible types, both have lively minds and buoyant dispositions.

Conic with psychic. A fair chance of agreement here as both are creative and sensitive. Probably the best combination as far as the psychic is concerned because the conic would at least provide a more realistic approach to life for them both.

Spatulate with spatulate. Good compatibility; both are restless and inventive so they would stimulate each other's imagination.

Spatulate with psychic. Another potentially disastrous combination.

Psychic with psychic. These two would certainly understand each other. They would be able to create a wonderful world of fantasy and fairy-tale around themselves but there would be little grasp of the realities in life. Would the shopping ever get done in this household or would the bills ever get paid, I wonder?

Level 2: Compatibility of Digit Types

The next step is to look at the fingers and thumbs and apply this information to the compatibility list below. See Chapter 4, 'Working from a Print' for finger lengths.

Long fingers with long fingers. Both would approach work in a careful, methodical way, patiently enjoying detail and minutiae. Perhaps there would be a little lack of spontaneity here though.

Short fingers with short fingers. Both would share a quick, instinctive and intuitive way of dealing with life. Possibly the finer points and details in the everyday running of things would simply go by the board or would not even be noticed at all.

Long fingers with short fingers. Excellent combination when able to work harmoniously together — potentially explosive otherwise. When they can work as a team the short-fingered person would be the wonderful organizer, splendid at making the plans and at setting up the projects. The long-fingered one can then take over to work out the refinements and fill in the details whilst the short fingers can move on to the next project in hand. When they don't see eye to eye it's because one is too fastidious whilst the other is too impulsive.

Lean fingers with fat fingers. Lean-fingered folk tend to be more spiritually inclined than their fatter-fingered-friends who are more earthy and materialistic. The lean fingers are able to tighten their belts philosophically when times are hard, whereas the fat fingers would suffer without their material security and touches of luxuries around them. Perhaps a little of lean's philosophy could help to ease life for the other during the rougher times and the fuller fingers could provide a touch of softness for their more ascetic friends.

Knuckled fingers with smooth fingers. These two might annoy each other. The smooth-fingered people consider the long deliberations of the others as frustrating and would often feel like shaking a response out of them. The knuckled-fingered people, however, might wish the others would stop to think a little before apparently recklessly opening their mouths.

Weak thumbs with strong thumbs. The stronger the thumb, the more strength of will and the more dominant the personality. The weaker the thumb the weaker the character. So, those with the stronger thumbs could use their forcefulness and dominance over the other, less determined types. Of course, it's quite possible that those with the weaker thumbs might prefer to be led and guided along by the others, especially so if they also lack confidence in themselves.

Digits widely spread with digits tightly closed. The wider spread denotes a more open-minded and extroverted personality, whereas the other is more withdrawn, reserved and introverted. Problems here would manifest themselves with the former being open, generous and socially gregarious whilst the latter is critical, suspicious and tenacious.

Level 3: Finger Print Compatibility

Now is the time to superimpose all the information collected regarding the skin patterning. Reference should be made to Chapter 5, 'Finger Print Patterns', in order to check and establish individual finger prints.

Whorls with loop patterns. Whorls are the most fixed of all the pattern types and extremely slow to make up their minds. The loops, however, are quick, intuitive and need change for stimulation. Consequently, these two could really rub each other up the wrong way. It would only be the flexibility and pliant nature of the loops that would save the day here.

Whorls with arches. A good combination. The arches are so good-natured that they could put up with anything and the whorls could feel quite comfortable with the arched types knowing that their individualistic approach to life would not be challenged.

Whorls with composites. These would get on because each takes time in the decision-making process. The fixity of the whorl could help the composite to become more decisive.

Loops with arches. A wonderfully gentle relationship.

Loops with composites. Not at all bad together. Both are fairly mutable and each would be prepared to understand the other.

Arches with composites. Again, an understanding and sympathetic pair.

Level 4: Heart Line Compatibility

Finally to complete the picture, it is time to overlay any information seen on the lines. When it comes to relationships it is obviously the heart line which will reveal most about an individual's emotions.

Rising up to between the 1st and 2nd fingers. This formation, as seen in Figure 131a, shows warm and generous emotions, but these people find it

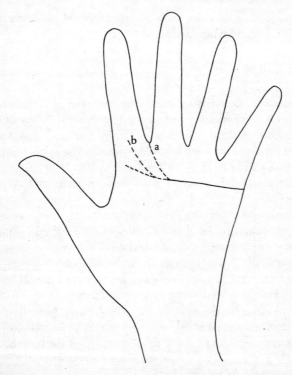

Figure 131

difficult to express their feelings in words. They tend, instead, to make their emotions known through their kind and loving actions.

Rising to the Mount of Jupiter. These are the idealistic types who tend to be unrealistic about relationships (Figure 131b). They see love and marriage through rose-tinted spectacles and relish dreams of romance, of knight errants and courtly love. Because of this idealism they can easily get hurt as they are so vulnerable. The higher the line climbs up the mount, the more jealous and possessive the person becomes.

Straight across towards the thumb edge. Work comes first with these people (Figure 131c) and everything or everyone else must fit in around it. So be prepared to take second place if you are hitched up to one of these!

Straight but ending under the middle finger. Rather more sexual desire and libido here than true loving kindness.

Happy Families

It is not commonly known that various characteristics of the hand are passed down from generation to generation, just as the colour of the eyes, for example, or similar noses might be inherited. The fact that one boy may get on better with his older sister than with his younger brother, or that a child has a closer relationship with her granny than with her mother may be explained, and therefore better understood, by a comparison of the hands of the members of a family. This is a most fascinating and absorbing exercise as it not only brings to light the network of relationships within the family, but it also gives a glimpse into the variety and complexity of genetic inheritance.

By working through the four levels outlined above it should be possible to ascertain the reasons why certain members get on better with others or why, indeed, some simply don't seem to hit it off at all. It is interesting to discover which child has inherited more characteristics from the paternal hand and which bears more of the maternal patterns. Figures 132a and 132b are prints of the right hands of a father and his son. Notice how they share a similar head line — so alike that even the island showing a period of worry and self-doubt

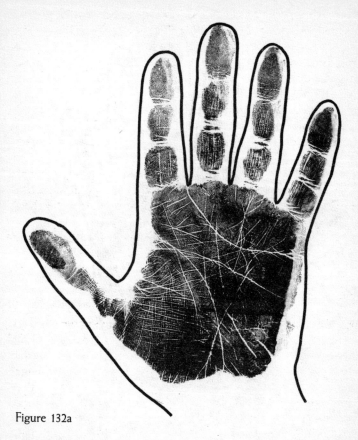

Figure 132a

from about 35 to 40 in the father's hand is matched in that of the youngster. Such similar features would denote a common understanding, a shared perception of life but only on an intellectual level. Emotionally, though, these two are not at all alike, as seen by the differences in the heart line — the father being much more demonstrative, expressive and easy-going, whilst the son appears cooler because of his extremely high standards of excellence.

More fascinating still is to find the child who has one hand which resembles that of the father, and the other, that of the mother. If, let's say, the objective hand takes after the father, then that child will appear to behave, think and possibly even look like him. The subjective hand,

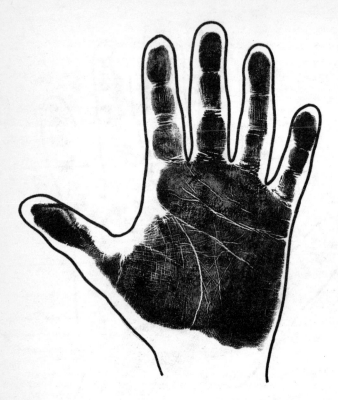

Figure 132b

though, resembling that of the mother, would denote that, emotionally, the child would be much more like her. The product, then, would be a real mixture of the two parents.

In the same way similarities, or otherwise, between the hands of brothers and sisters will highlight the reasons why some seem to live quite happily together whilst others simply argue and bicker, some even, for the rest of their lives!

This sort of exercise should provide a better insight into the character and personality of each member of the family and, even if it doesn't change the emotional feelings each bears towards the other, it should, at least, help to further a deeper understanding between them.

Friends and Colleagues

The sort of people we are drawn into friendship with are, generally speaking, people like ourselves, those who think like us, have similar types of life-styles and who, in the broadest sense, share our own philosophy and outlook on life.

When comparing and contrasting hands with friends, work through the four levels outlined above but, in addition, consider also the head line, which will give clues about the way we think, about our preoccupations and intellectual abilities.

The Head Line

1. The straighter the line across the palm, the more logical, down-to-earth, practical and pragmatic the individual. Sciences, technology, business or commerce would suit.
2. The more curved the line, the more creative, artistic, broader-minded and expansive the mentality.
3. A line which begins straight to the centre and then curves downwards denotes a combination of pragmatism and creativity.
4. An exceedingly steep curve suggests an over-active imagination, possibly moody and, in the extreme, a danger of becoming manic-depressive.
5. A forked head line may indicate real estate, literary, or financial acumen when the branch is situated under the middle, ring or little fingers respectively.
6. A Simian line denotes intensity, concentration and probably an obsessional mind.

When it comes to bosses, colleagues and work-associates it may not be possible or feasible to actually study their hands at length lest one be considered forward, inquisitive or just plain crazy! In these circumstances, then, one must simply resort to sneaking a glance at their hands whenever the situation presents itself. Even in this way, quite a lot of useful information may be gleaned.

Certainly working through Levels 1 and 2 would be possible as just a glance is needed to determine whether a hand is square or psychic in shape. A quick look to see if the fingers are long, short, smooth or knuckled would also reveal the degree of compatibility.

When it comes to bosses or superiors, an assessment of thumbs would instantly show the strength of character and thus indicate how one should best relate to them. For instance, if you notice long second phalanges then only articulate, cogent arguments will wash, but if the whole digit is short and squat, then for heaven's sake stay out of the way if you see the storm clouds gathering!

Unfortunately, unless a closer inspection of the hand is carried out then Levels 3 and 4 must go by the board. If it is at all possible, though, check the finger prints, especially on the indices, because those who have whorls there like things done their way and moreover like to be in charge. The heart line, of course, would reveal people's aspirations and expectations, would tell of compassionate understanding and, by the way, would also highlight the 'office wolf'.

Partners and Lovers

When it comes to working out our personal or romantic attachments, obviously running through the four levels will not only reveal how we ourselves relate to our partners, but also how they respond to us. The heart lines, particularly, should be compared and contrasted but so too should the head lines because the way we think about ourselves, about others and about the world in general, plays an essential part in the way we formulate our relationships.

There are, however, other lines which give specific clues regarding marriage and love affairs and these are the fate, influence and partnership lines.

Branches which rise from the mount of Luna and then join the fate line are recognized signs of relationships and are known as influence lines. It is the structure of these lines, together with the effect they have on the fate line itself, which describes the nature and quality of the relationship in question. If the line is broken or islanded (Figure 133a) then the relationship is rather troublesome and fraught with difficulties. Should it later strengthen then those difficulties would have been surmounted. If the line actually merges with the main fate line (Figure 133b), the point of union is regarded as the time when the relationship actually consolidates itself, in either marriage or firm commitment of some kind. But, if the line doesn't actually touch (Figure

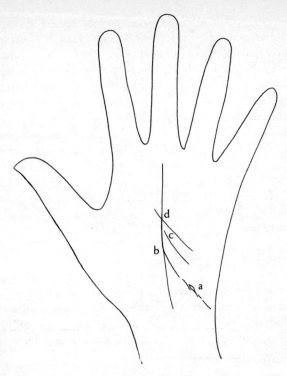

Figure 133

133c) or, indeed, if it crosses over the fate line (Figure 133d), this is considered a rather disastrous or unhappy ending to the affair. Such a sign might exist, for example, if a marriage is called off right at the last minute.

It is quite possible to time these events by reading off the scale on the fate line as illustrated in Chapter 8, 'Time On Our Hands'.

The quality of the fate line after the appearance of an influence line reveals the effects that the relationship has on the subject. If the main line continues strongly, then it can be said that the relationship has a positive effect. Should the line become even stronger than before then the whole effect would be one of improvement and amelioration.

Conversely, though, if the fate line worsens, either by showing islands, fading or fraying, or if it is cut by crossing bars, then it would imply

Figure 134

that the relationship brings with it problems, complications and opposition. If, after the union of the influence line, the fate line should break and a whole new section begins (Figure 134), this would show that the relationship has led to a completely new and different way of life for the people concerned.

Figure 135

Sometimes, a line may be seen rising from the Luna mount and, instead of joining the fate line, running along parallel to it. Such a formation as this invariably indicates an excellent relationship but one which is more like a partnership. Indeed, business partnerships are sometimes marked out like this in the hand too.

Relationship lines can also occur inside the life line and parallel to it (Figure 135). The stronger the line the more important the relationship, although the length of it does not necessarily indicate the duration of the relationship itself, but gives lots of clues regarding the influence it has on the subject.

It used to be said that marriage lines were seen lying horizontally on the percussion edge of the hand just below the little finger. Investigation has not proved this theory correct as in many cases several of these lines exist on the hands of individuals who have only enjoyed a single life-long marriage. I have noticed, however, that on some hands an extension of one of these lines, across the top of the palm and cutting the heart line, has represented the tragic bereavement of a dearly beloved partner (Figure 136).

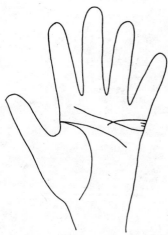

Figure 136

Equally erroneous, it would appear, is the idea that vertical bars, cutting through these so-called marriage lines represent children. Many such bars have been observed on the hands of people who have never had any children of their own but who have been somehow attached to youngsters in their lives — teachers, for instance, might have these markings, or favourite aunts and uncles. If looking for signs of children in the hand, it is possible to detect their appearance as tiny branches which drop down from the inside of the life line (Figure 137). Once again, it is possible to date these events and influences according to the time scale on the life line itself.

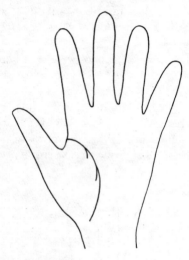

Figure 137

CHAPTER TEN

Success and Happiness

The concepts of success and happiness are deeply personal, for what amounts to a successful achievement for one individual may not at all fit the bill for another. The flush of success that a hard-worked-for degree might bring to one young person would be meaningless to another who doesn't prize educational achievements at all. The excitement of landing an important property deal for one man would just leave cold another for whom literary accomplishments might be the ultimate goal in life.

Nevertheless, bearing in mind the individualistic notion of success there are various signs and markings all over the hand which point to such times of triumph in the subject's life.

The very first factor to be considered here is the actual structure of the main lines. Islanded, chained or broken lines are not conducive to a sense of happiness and well-being as these imply worry, interference or opposition to one's aims. In fact, heavily chained lines might even suggest that the health of the individual is not quite up to scratch and as such would contribute little to feelings of success. So, good clear lines which are well-engraved in the palm are the first indications of the potential for a happy and successful life.

Success lines are, in fact seen all over, more usually as branches rising from the main lines of head, life and fate. In general terms, the anomalous lines which rise upwards are favourable whilst those which cut the hand horizontally imply obstruction and impediments.

Branches off the Head Line

Starting with the head line as it travels beneath the index finger, then, any branch shooting upwards to the mount of Jupiter denotes academic success. Passing important school exams, for example, might be recorded in this way. I remember seeing just such a branch occurring on the hand of a young scientist at around his 26th year but the branch itself bore a large island in it. The branch did indeed represent academic success in the form of a higher degree which he strove hard to attain — working and supporting a young family whilst studying at night and in his limited spare time. The island, though, represented his disenchantment on finding that the eventual degree did not open out the sorts of opportunities for him that he had been led to expect.

A branch rising from the head line up towards the middle finger often suggests a feeling of achievement within the subject's career. Promotion, for instance, might be seen in this way.

Branches to the Apollo mount under the ring finger, or to the Apollo line itself, represent creative successes, possibly achievements in the world of the arts, sometimes accompanied by financial rewards but more usually implying a deep feeling of self-fulfilment in this way.

As the area under the little finger is concerned with business, commerce and financial affairs a branch in this direction would denote a successful outcome in any of these fields. I have seen an example of this sort of line on the hand of a lady who, after her family had grown up and left home, went into business on her own. Initially, she worked from home, taking in any secretarial work she could, but soon she had so much work that she was able to expand and set up a small secretarial business of her own, employing several other people under her. It was the successful expansion of her business that was represented by the branch shooting off to the Mercury mount.

Branches off the Fate Line

Similarly, branches rising from the fate line towards the mounts bear the same sort of interpretation except that these refer more specifically to achievements connected with the career, whereas those from the head line emphasize the intellectual side of personal endeavour.

It is perhaps unusual to find a branch from the base of the fate line shooting up to the index mount and thus expecting it to represent academic successes. More usual would be those branches which rise from higher up on this line and leading to that area, in which case they might represent times of career achievements within the realms of religion, politics or the law. One example of this which springs to mind was on the hand of a man who gave up his career in mid-stream in order to devote himself to a life in local politics.

Again, as the normal course of this line is to the Saturn mount, it would be uncommon for it to throw branches out into this area. However, should they occur, they might suggest two jobs or preoccupations or a secondary interest which runs concurrently with the main career or way of life of the individual.

A branch rising from the fate line to the Apollo mount might indeed be the Sun line itself. If an independent line of Sun exists then this feature can be read as a branch, in which case it would indicate the time at which the subjects felt they had reached that point of satisfaction and creative fulfilment in their work and in their lives.

Branches from the fate line to the Mercury mount under the little finger can, like those from the head line, mean expansion into business, commercial or financial affairs. This feature on a scientific hand, however, can also indicate successes in the medical or technological fields. In addition to this, if there is a long, elegant little finger, together with other signs of creativity in the hand, then it might be quite possible that a branch in this direction could well indicate literary achievements too.

Branches off the Life Line

Branches may also rise from the life line up towards the fingers but in these instances it is important that they do, in fact, actually stem from the very line itself and then push their way upwards. It is so easy to confuse such lines with ones that begin just inside the life line, and which might therefore represent emotional upheaval, rather than the much happier indication of success. Rising branches from the life line stand for personal endeavours, the feeling of having succeeded, sometimes against the odds, of having surmounted obstacles or difficulties, of having attained a long-held wish or of having reached one's goal through hard work.

From the top of the line, branches which rise to the index mount denote, like those off the head line, academic achievements usually gained through hard work.

When a branch occurs which reaches up to the Saturn mount below the middle finger this can mean a major step forward in the individual's life. Sometimes this may entail an important move, perhaps a larger property or the house of one's dreams. Or it can even suggest a brand new start in life, a sweeping away of everything that is restricting and limiting, and beginning again almost like a rebirth. There is, here, the feeling of struggle or of hard work but the promise that the individual will eventually succeed in overcoming the difficulties.

Both of these examples were clearly illustrated in the hands of two ladies whom I can recall distinctly. One had, with her husband, built up through her life first one and then a second grocery store. They worked all hours to make these shops successful knowing that their eventual dream was to sell them in order to take on a restaurant and country club. The strong branch reaching up to the Saturn mount, then, indicated the crowning glory of their endeavours when they eventually bought the very business they had worked for all their lives.

The second example occurred in the hand of a lady who had, for years, put up with a very unhappy marriage 'because of the children'. In her case this strong branch represented the start of a new, independent life when, the children having grown up, she was able to leave her husband and thus free herself from the years of distress she had suffered.

Branches which rise from the life line to the Apollo mount below the ring finger denote that the individual's talents are recognized and rewarded at that time. Often creative people, those in the public eye or in the media may possess this feature when they finally 'make it to the top'.

Branches from the life line to the Mercury mount under the little finger will illustrate successful personal achievements, through the individual's hard work, in such fields as business, commerce, technology, science or literature.

Occasionally, tiny rising branches may be seen off this line which are not long enough to actually reach any of the mounts. In every case, these will denote a feeling of success, even if it's in a minor way, but will be, nevertheless, strong enough and important enough to be registered in the subject's hand. If several of these tiny branches are seen in succession they suggest a period of growth in the subject's life, when each small achievement adds to a general feeling of contentment and well-being.

The Sun or Apollo Line

The Sun line is, perhaps, the most well-known of the indications of success and happiness. This can also be called the Apollo line as it lies vertically in the hand and sweeps up in the direction of the ring finger. Although it is generally considered a sign of success it does, in actual fact, represent a sense of satisfaction and fulfilment in whatever way that applies to the particular individual.

If, for instance, motherhood should bring that sense of fulfilment, then the Sun line would develop on that hand at the time that feeling was realized. On a different hand, the line might be read as indicating peace of mind after a long period of emotional problems. Yet again, it is possible that the Sun line could stand for public acclaim. So, it can be seen that the line has several interpretations according to the individual hand that is being analysed but generally it highlights improvement and a better sense of well-being in the whole quality of the subject's life.

This line may begin at any point in the hand but it must push its way up to the Apollo mount. If the line is long and strong, commencing down near the wrist, then the individual is likely to achieve success from a very early age. Although this feature is rare, it does exist in the hands of those who might be called 'child stars'. Obviously, then, it tells of the sunny and charismatic personality and disposition which would bring that person into prominence at such an early age.

A line beginning on the Luna mount and sweeping up to Apollo shows public favour and recognition. An actor might have this marking but so too might a favoured politician or indeed anyone in the public eye.

Beginning higher up, above the heart line, this formation suggests that the sense of true happiness and contentment begins much later on in life, often in retirement, but it is a splendid augury for an old age filled with warmth, love and understanding.

When there are several parallel Sun lines it may denote a person who has many diverse interests and who takes great pleasure in all of them. It might be said that these people may never become successful in anything in particular as they divide and scatter their attention instead of channelling and concentrating it into one major objective. If, however, this is their way of deriving satisfaction and fulfilment then surely this must be success enough for them.

Three lines commencing above the heart line have quite a different interpretation. This formation is seen on the hands of those who seem to be fairly lucky when it comes to money. It doesn't necessarily mean that they will become out and out rich but that, whenever they need money, it just seems to appear, even at the very last minute. Whether it is that they are 'born lucky' or simply that they have a 'knack' with money is unclear. Certainly the message for these people is that they shouldn't worry about money, for when they need it something invariably 'turns up'.

Figure 138

Obviously, the stronger the line, the better the expression of success or happiness. But, should the line be broken, fragmented or intermittent then it would show that these feelings are rather spasmodic and come in fits and starts. Traditional palmistry states that an island seen in the Sun line (Figure 138) reveals a scandal, and possibly in some cases this might be true. The idea of getting a 'bad press' through this time, for example, could be represented in this way in the hand. Generally, though, such a formation would suggest a period of disenchantment or dissatisfaction. The composition of the line after this event would tell how the individual overcomes the difficulties implied: if the line strengthens again then the reputation or peace of mind is restored. But, if the line should then break up, it would tell that the difficulties indicated have left a marked detrimental effect on that individual.

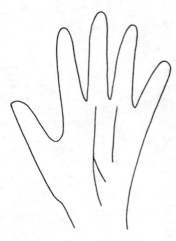

Figure 139

The fascinating part of analysing this line is to compare and contrast it with other events and markings elsewhere on the hand. Invariably, the development of the Sun line coincides with other features which reveal the reason for its growth. For example, if the line should begin to grow at the same time that a large island on the head line comes to an end, then it can be assumed that the individual has come through a period of worry and indecision and has found direction and satisfaction. Should the growth coincide with a marriage, as illustrated in Figure 139, or a move or a birth, then it would be these events which bring deep contentment to that individual. Perhaps a new section of fate line is seen, or a rising branch off the head line, in which case it can be confirmed that any changes taking place within the occupation will be for the better.

Likewise, adverse events can be checked off on this line too. For instance, if an island exists in the Sun line it could coincide with a broken influence line, thus revealing that a troublesome relationship is responsible for the individual's unhappiness. Perhaps, if a break in the Sun line is seen at the same time as an island in the life line (Figure 140), then it could be that an illness is taking its toll and marring the individual's sense of contentment in life.

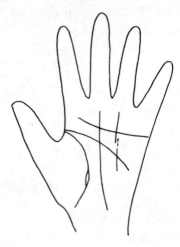

Figure 140

So, always match the point of origin of this line, also mapping its construction and composition, to the rest of the indications seen and the pieces of the jig-saw should soon come together. In this way it is possible to construct a clear picture of the progress of the individual's success and ideas of happiness and contentment.

The Star

When three little lines cross on a particular spot, the formation created is called a star. There are two positions in the hand where the occurrence of a star is especially significant with regard to success and happiness. Firstly, one found on the Jupiter mount, under the index finger (Figure 141a), highlights a strong potential to succeed in whatever area the individual should choose. This indeed is a most favourable marking to possess. Secondly, one on the Apollo mount, below the ring finger (Figure 141b), suggests the sort of accomplishments which could take

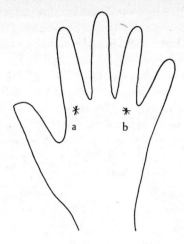

Figure 141

the individual into the public eye and, sometimes, even fame. Both these markings certainly enhance and increase the chances of finding personal happiness and success.

One of the most important ways of attaining true contentment is in fulfilling one's potential. All too often, people lose their sense of direction, lack confidence in themselves and in their abilities or feel there is something drawing them but don't know what that might be. By analysing the hand it is possible to highlight areas of excellence, to guide the individuals by showing them their strengths and weaknesses, revealing their latent gifts and talents. For example, to realize that a square exists on the Jupiter mount could confirm a person's hidden desire to become a teacher. Equally, pointing out the medical stigmata might re-evoke that childhood dream to become a doctor, a nurse, a vet or a healer. Describing powers of creativity seen on a hand may steer the individual into successfully expressing artistic talents.

In many cases it is not realistic to expect that such revelations would make the individuals suddenly quit their jobs, turn their backs on their former lives and start all over again. It would be impractical, let's say, for a middle-aged man with a growing family to decide, on the strength of a hand analysis, to drop everything and embark on years of training in order to fulfil a life-long ambition to become a doctor. Nor indeed would it be practicable for a mother to abandon her family and home and go off to the Third World in order to satisfy a vocational need to help others.

The realistic use for outlining potential is that it can indeed, in some cases, encourage and guide the individual into a better alternative occupation or way of life but, much more often, it can help to stimulate and promote interests or hobbies which provide the sort of satisfaction and fulfilment that the subjects seek but cannot find in the normal course of their jobs or daily lives.

CHAPTER ELEVEN

Health

There is no doubt that hand analysis can be used as a valuable aid in medical diagnosis. The hand itself can be treated as a map, rich in potential indicators of good and bad health. These indicators act as an excellent early warning system, showing how the body's weak links can, through time, develop into clinical disease. Such indicators can be detected and picked up in the hand at an early stage so that the subject can take preventive action, and, if possible, avoid the condition becoming a chronic disorder.

There are three basic areas from which the trained eye will piece together the various clues relating to health matters. The first is seen in the temperature and colour of the hand itself and in the condition of the nails. The second area lies in the nature, construction and formation of the lines, both major and minor ones. And the third area is centred on an analysis of the dermatoglyphics, the actual patterning and condition of the skin ridges which cover the entire palm and fingers.

Colour and Temperature of the Hand

When assessing the colour and temperature of the hand it must always be compared to the ambient temperature of the room — a hot hand on a hot day should not be mistakenly considered a potential hyperthyroid case, for example. Equally, the activity of the subjects immediately prior to reading the hand should also be noted, for hands that drip with perspiration might show that their owners had been running for a bus just as easily as they might suggest allergic sensitivities.

Having carefully noted these details then, an otherwise cold feel to the hand could indicate poor circulation and, if it also has a bluish tinge, this could suggest the possibilities of cardiovascular irregularities.

Hot, red hands often denote a feverish disposition but if they are noticeably dry and rough this might allude to hypothyroid activity (under-active) whereas, hot and wet with perspiration, could suggest an over-active thyroid. Sometimes, the hands may also be hot and clammy if the subjects are sensitive to certain allergenics.

Extremely white hands may be a sign of anaemia whilst a tinge of yellow, other than on a sallow complexion or a fading tan, can denote jaundice, biliousness or any such liverish complaint.

The Nails

The nails are often a good indicator of the state of one's health. On average, nails take about six months to grow from the base to the top of the pink, or quick, as it is sometimes called. In this way, if any ridging, pitting or spotting of the nail is seen, which might imply illness or dietary deficiencies, it is possible to date the occurrence of those events. For example, if tiny dents exist about two-thirds of the way up the nail, then it would show that about four months ago the diet was somewhat poor and nutritionally out of balance.

On a European hand, nails should be of a pinkish colour with good, clear moons at the base. If they are rather white they may be indicating an anaemic condition. Very red nails suggest not only a fiery temper but hot-bloodedness too, which could be due to too much iron. Bluish nails tell of poor oxygenation and could be an indication of pulmonary or cardiac weakness. Another indication of weaknesses of the heart and lungs may be shown by the moons, which can be overly large, sometimes taking up half the size of the quick or, alternatively, almost non-existent. Nails with a tendency to curve around the tips of the fingers may also denote a poor oxygen supply to the lungs — a condition which is often seen in the hands of smokers or those who have recently given up.

Mineral deficiencies and that feeling of being run down, are both readily reflected in the nails. Sometimes this is seen by an overlarge cuticle and at other times by the appearance of little white spots which indicate an imbalance of calcium. Any pitting, or tiny dents, horizontal ridging or nails which are dished or concave all denote dietary problems or a lack of the essential minerals and vitamins necessary for good health. Flaking or easily broken nails are another reflection of this condition. Accidents or sudden shocks to the system, however, may also be represented on the nail by horizontal ridges, so it is of vital importance that other features, such as the lines, should be consulted for confirmation and corroboration before formulating any conclusions on the individual's state of health.

Whereas horizontal ridging can illustrate poor nutrition, vertical ridging is quite different as this tends to highlight allergic sensitivities. This is invariably accompanied, and thus confirmed, by the presence of the Via Lascivia, otherwise known as the poison or allergy line.

The Lines

For best effect, lines should be well engraved and solid along their course. Any breaks suggest either physiological or psychological changes according to the line itself. Islands denote worry, anxiety or self-doubts if seen on the head, fate or heart lines or, if on the life line, they might indicate ill health or a weakening of physical strength. Chaining suggests mineral deficiencies or chemical imbalances and should be further investigated in order to correct the condition implied.

Dermatoglyphics

Modern research in the medical field is beginning to throw important and exciting new light on skin patterning. Firstly, studies are confirming that finger and palm prints are inherited. But secondly, they are also showing that any hiccups during the formation of the embryo or foetus will be directly translated onto the skin patterns, so any genetic or congenital malformations will be mapped onto the palms of the hands and soles of the feet. In particular, the research is establishing a link between certain epidermal patterns and pathological conditions such as Down's Syndrome, Turner's syndrome and Klinefelter's syndrome, all of which are due to congenital defects and chromosomal abnormalities. Other conditions such as autism and childhood schizophrenia, for example, are also being examined in this light.

What the research seems to be indicating is that there are significant differences in the skin patterns between those with these sorts of conditions, or syndromes, and the patterns seen in the hands of normal people. In general, finger prints are of less complexity than in the normal hand with perhaps more arches, especially so in autistic children. In addition, skin ridges may be poorly formed or broken up more than usual. In the case of Mongolism, or Down's Syndrome, a higher proportion of patterns were found on the hypothenar, or mount of Luna, and a significantly greater number of radial loops were found on the 3rd and 4th finger tips.

Studies have also been carried out on the hands of parents of abnormal children with a view to facilitate prediction of possible genetic problems. Further research, however, needs to be conducted in this area so that dermatoglyphics may be recognized as an aid to genetic counselling in the future.

The Healthy Hand

Ideally, the healthy hand is one which is of an even temperature and, in the European hand, of a good pinkish hue. The nails should be free from horizontal or vertical ridges, pittings or coloured specks, and also of a pinkish tinge, with creamy-coloured moons. All the skin ridges should be clear and sharp and the finger prints should not be obscured by crossing lines on the finger tips. The major and minor lines should be present, well-engraved and clearly defined. The fewer islands, chains, cross-bars or other adverse markings the better, both for the physical and psychological well-being of the individual.

Stress and Tension

Indicators of stress and tension may be compiled from four different areas in the hand: from the finger tips, the number of lines, the quality of cross bars on the life line and shape of the percussion edge. Figure 142 epitomizes the stressed hand.

Horizontal lines lying across the finger tips are the prime indicators of stress. The crux of the problem or anxiety is denoted by the greater concentration of lines on particular fingers. If more horizontal dashes are seen on the index, the problems concern the subject's ego and

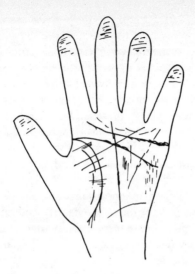

Figure 142

standing in the world. On the middle finger, these would suggest anxieties regarding career matters but also it might be felt that one's sense of security was threatened in some way. More lines concentrated on the Apollo finger would show discontentment and disillusionment when it comes to the individual's feelings of self-fulfilment and happiness. On the little finger these are connected with self-expression and sometimes specifically with sexual problems. If lots of lines are seen on the thumb tip it would show that the problems are having an adverse effect on the individual's nervous system.

It would be simple indeed if these lines existed on individual fingers alone in such a way that the whole nature of the problem was revealed at a glance. More often than not, though, what tends to happen is that our problems spill over into all the other areas of our lives so that all the finger tips receive a smattering of the stress lines to a greater or lesser degree. It is, then, the finger which has the greatest number of these lines which holds the key. Sometimes, it might even be a combination of finger tips as in the case, for instance, when both the middle and ring fingers seem to be covered. Here, it would suggest that happiness and home life (that is, the sense of security) are on shaky ground possibly because of family, marital or financial problems. Once the areas of concern have been established in this way, an analysis of the lines in the rest of the hand should provide the reasons for the existing problems.

Because the lines on the objective hand change quicker than those on the subjective one it is even possible to detect at what stage the problems have reached. If more finger tips are covered in lines on the objective hand than on its corresponding one then it is fair to say that the problems have recently set in. When both sets of finger tips show an equal amount of lines the problems have reached a climax. Then, as the situation is resolved, the lines on the objective hand start to disappear whilst those on the subjective hand remain for a little longer until they, too, finally clear away.

Sometimes, these lines can appear fairly rapidly, perhaps within a few days, particularly so if the individual has been suffering from strain, overworking or taking on more responsibility than usual but the lines should just as quickly disappear once the normal balance or pressure of work has been restored.

The horizontal lines on the finger tips are the first obvious signs that the individual is, or has recently been, suffering from the effects of stress. But another prime indicator which shows, at a glance, whether a person is indeed prone to tension is the full or empty hand.

The difference between the full and empty hand is that one is covered in lines, rather like a cobweb effect, whilst the other simply has the barest minimum. The more lines there are, the more sensitive the individual, so people with the full hand tend to worry and to be more anxious than most. Those with the empty hand, though, seem rarely to have a day's illness for it's as if they're blithely unaware that they even possess a nervous system at all! These people, then, are more able and more likely to shrug off the everyday anxieties which the fuller-handed folk would tend to allow to build up into potentially stressful situations. So, when it comes to stress, always be aware that it will be those with the fuller hand who have the disadvantage here for they are more prone to fretfulness from the outset.

Indeed, fretfulness which can lead to stress and tension may also be represented in two other ways. Firstly, this can be seen by many fine lines crossing the main life line. Usually, strong bars across this line signify emotional upheavals but if several fine hair lines are bunched together this signifies, not a series of distressing incidents as might at first appear, but rather a nature which is disposed to nervous worry.

The second indication is seen in the actual construction of the percussion edge of the hand. A palm which noticeably bows outwards just under the little finger denotes what I call a fidgety mentality. People with this formation have the sort of minds which are constantly working, constantly thinking and racing ahead. They simply can't sit still for a minute without planning what they're going to do tomorrow, next weekend, next month. In fact, this is a good sign of highly strung individuals who tend to live on their nerves. This characteristic mental drive does warn that they should be aware of not over-taxing their physical resources too much lest they end up physically and mentally exhausted.

A good recommendation in this case would be that they find an absorbing interest or hobby which is totally relaxing both for the mind and the body. Simple yoga practice or relaxation exercises could help a great deal to restore calm and tranquillity before stress and tension set in.

Allergies

Individual sensitivity to particular foodstuffs, chemicals, drugs, etc., is certainly a most interesting study and one which requires much more medical attention and research than it is at present enjoying. Although some of the more common forms of allergy, such as hay fever, have been recognized for some time, interest in the wider mechanism, causes and cures of allergies is growing and people are now more ready to accept that conditions which were once thought to be neurotic, psychosomatic, strangely recurring but inexplicable, might indeed be due to simple allergic reactions.

It has recently been established, for instance, that certain types of food colouring have been responsible for hyperactivity in some children — a condition which hitherto had been thought of as a behavioural problem to be treated with firmer discipline or with psychiatric care.

The fact that we may sometimes, for no apparent reason, feel a bit low, undergo a sudden change of mood, perspire more than usual, have palpitations of the heart, get a little breathless or whatever, could be explained by the fact that our systems are reacting to substances with which they cannot cope or which have an adverse effect on us. The difficulty lies in isolating that substance or allergen and thereafter either avoiding it altogether in our daily lives or desensitizing ourselves to it. This, of course, can be a very long process and in most cases requires professional attention.

Alas, the hand gives no instant magic formulae with which to pinpoint these allergens but what it can do is to show, quite clearly, those who are potentially susceptible to this sort of sensitivity. Simply to be able to detect those who are sensitive in this way must surely be of great benefit as it alerts them to any possible reactions they may have experienced and yet been unable to explain.

Figure 143

Basically there are two areas in the hand which point to allergic sensitivity and these are the nails and the Via Lascivia. Nails which are strongly ridged vertically are the first signs of such potential sensitivity and this can then be confirmed by the presence of the Via Lascivia (Figure 143). This is a line which is seen at the base of the palm usually lying across the mount of Luna. It used to be thought that it represented some rather unsavoury character traits but now this theory has been debunked and modern hand analysis recognizes it as the poison or allergy line. When both these features are present in a hand, then, it would seem that the individual is indeed potentially subject to adverse reactions to chemicals, alcohol, drugs or whatever.

Eyes, Teeth and Ears

Any problems connected with eyes, teeth or ears are detected on, or above, the heart line. An island in this line immediately under the ring finger (Figure 144a) often suggests problems with sight and anyone with this formation would be wise to have their eyes checked. A patch of fine hair lines situated below the ring and little fingers and lying just above the heart line (Figure 144b) often signifies that dental attention

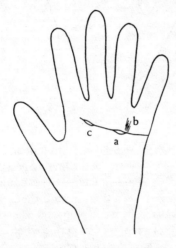

Figure 144

is necessary. Lastly, another island in the line, but this time below the index or middle fingers (Figure 144c), may denote problems with hearing and so it is recommended that this, too, should be checked out as early as possible. This is especially important because hearing defects can be difficult to detect and can often impede a youngster's educational development if they go uncorrected for any length of time.

Headaches

Headaches, dizziness, lack of concentration can all be seen on the head line itself. Migraine, the most notorious of the headache group, is represented by tiny indentations in the line which appear almost like

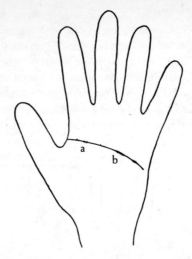

Figure 145

little white specks when the line is stretched (Figure 145a). A concentration of these anywhere on the line suggests recurring bouts of this condition and so, if timed accurately, it could be possible to take some sort of preventive action to ward them off.

If the line itself broadens out at any point and takes on a rather fuzzy appearance (Figure 145b) it represents a period when clarity of thought is lacking, when there is a marked loss of concentration and possibly some dizziness too. These conditions could be due to anxieties and worry as a result of work pressures or emotional upheavals, or indeed there could be a clinical reason such as sinusitis as the root cause. Whatever is the underlying problem, confirmation would be shown elsewhere on the hand perhaps in the form of a trauma line, in the first instance or, in the latter case, islands in the life line.

Mineral Deficiencies

Mineral imbalances show up on the nails either in the form of white specks which could be suggestive of a calcium deficiency or, by the fact that the nails are brittle, split easily, grow discoloured or distorted.

Unfortunately, except in the case of calcium, these imbalances have not yet been researched thoroughly enough to be able to state with total certainty which specific minerals are represented in the hand. Nevertheless, a heavily islanded heart line or strongly chained head line would broadly indicate mineral or chemical deficiencies which could then be investigated further should the individual deem it necessary.

However, anaemia is instantly seen if the palm is stretched and the main lines, rather than being a healthy pink colour, appear to be white or washed out altogether. This is a sign of a lack of iron and often occurs on women's hands after menstruation or on those who generally feel run down.

The Cardiovascular System

It is the colour of the nails that first gives the clue to any irregularities of the vascular system. A deep bluish tinge, especially around the base of the nail, is often the sign of poor circulation, and so too are hands which are generally cold. A bright red hue to the nails can indicate an irascible temper, the sort of temperament, it was traditionally said, that could lead to apoplexy or strokes.

The heart line is the obvious area to analyse when looking into

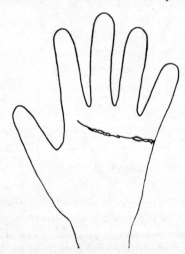

Figure 146

cardiovascular problems although it must be stressed here that, again, not enough research has been carried out to verify the theories put forward concerning this line. However, it is possible that islands, chaining, fraying of the line or a complete break could denote a predisposition to cardiac problems (Figure 146). Sometimes, it has been observed, a concentration of tiny specks formed around an island in this line may indicate the possibility of angina pectoris but, as this has not yet been confirmed satisfactorily, all such indications should be treated as theoretical and not as proven fact.

The Reproductive System

Problems relating to the male and female reproductive systems are represented in two areas both located at the base of the palm. Firstly, a top rascette which markedly bows upwards and lies in an arch on the palm itself (Figure 147a) invariably denotes internal weaknesses more often than not of the reproductive system.

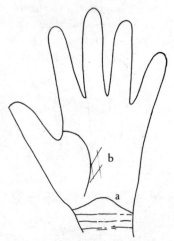

Figure 147

The second indication of a predisposition to complications here can be seen in a kite-shape formation lying about one-third of the way up from the wrist and attached to the outside of the life line (Figure

147b). When this formation is present it can warn of potential uro-genital problems in men and gynaecological complications in women, and this can range from anything to do with irregularities of the menstrual cycle right down to the possibility of a hysterectomy. If this sign does exist, then regular medical check-ups are advised as this is one of those excellent early warning signals of conditions which can be avoided if preventive action is taken.

Rheumatic Ailments

The effects of rheumatism and arthritis can be seen on the joints and knuckles of the hand and fingers which become painfully inflamed and distorted. (Figure 148 depicts the hand print of a lady who has

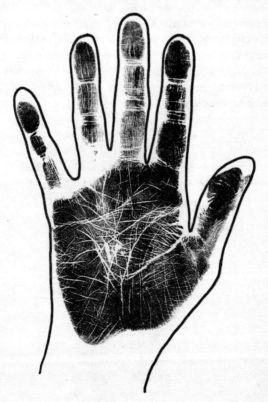

Figure 148

suffered from arthritis for many years.) One of the causes of these conditions is the bodily retention or poor elimination of uric acid. The build-up, over the years, of uric acid may be seen on the percussion side of the palm in the form of tiny hair lines lying obliquely over the mounts of Mars and Luna. Closer examination reveals that the fine lines are, in fact, a breaking down of the skin ridges and it is the extent of this veiling, as it is called, which tells of the degree of acidity in the system. Those who possess any signs of this type of veiling would be wise to check their diets and try to avoid too many acidy foods.

Digestive Disorders

Anyone who tends to suffer from problems of the digestive system or alimentary tract such as dyspepsia, intestinal acidity, nervous, fluttery or 'gippy tummy', for example, would invariably have a patch of fine hair lines right in the centre of the palm lying obliquely between the life and heart lines and clustering around the Mercury line, if it is present (Figure 149). The Mercury line itself would be twisted and ragged in this case. This feature is again a warning that the diet is poor or deficient and should be checked and corrected.

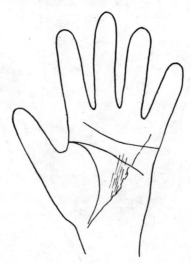

Figure 149

Other signs of poor nutrition can be seen in the nails, particularly if these are dished, pitted or have noticeable horizontal grooves in them. Such features are often seen on those who radically change their eating habits or who go on crash diets. As the nails take something like six months to grow, it is possible to detect when the effects of the poor diet took place.

The Respiratory Tract

Susceptibility to pulmonary problems, such as bronchitis, pneumonia, heavy colds and chesty coughs, is often represented by islands at the top of the life line, especially so if these occurred as childhood diseases (Figure 150). In addition, islands also seen in the Mercury line can confirm this predisposition. Few moons and nails which curve around the finger tips may be possible signs of weak lungs and poor oxygenation — a feature often seen in the hands of heavy smokers or those who have recently given up. Catarrhal inflammation or sinusitis problems are often characterized by tiny flecks in the main lines and particularly in that of the life line.

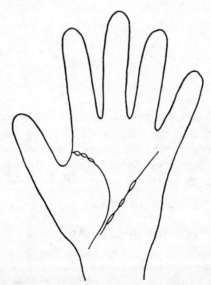

Figure 150

The Endocrine System

It has been suggested that any problems with the endocrine glands, the pituitary, pineal, thymus and thyroid, are indicated by vertical lines on the finger tips. Of these four glands I have only so far managed to confirm that hyperactivity of the thyroid is indeed marked by such lines on the tip of the little finger (Figure 151). Further study of the other glands and their problems needs to be carried out before applying them to their corresponding finger tips or other areas of the palm.

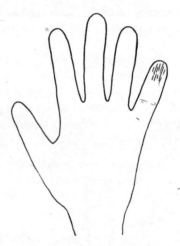

Figure 151

Despite the lack of concrete evidence, though, I do find that people who have all their finger tips covered in both horizontal and vertical lines are showing signs that their general health or body chemistry is out of balance. Often, they are mentally stressed and anxious whilst also physically at a low ebb and thus exposing themselves to ill health or disease.

Senility and Problems of Old Age

When considering the clinical problems of the elderly these fall into the two broad categories of physical and psychological ill health.

It is the last section of the life line which deals with retirement and

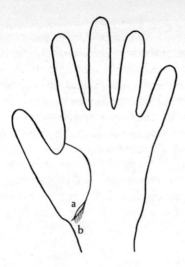

Figure 152

old age and, if this part of the line should be islanded (Figure 152a), then it is a sign that the health of the individual could be impaired through that time. Fine lines dropping down from the life line (Figure 152b) are also an indication of a general debility, a lack of physical

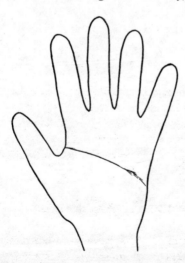

Figure 153

resources or a dissipation of energy which can lead to a lowering of resistance to disease. These potential indicators can be timed on the line and perhaps preventive measures sought to boost the individual's resources.

The psychological problems associated with old age such as senility and memory loss may be detected on the head line. Any island present on the last section of the line would show mental weakness and forgetfulness, whilst fraying, breaking or thinning out at the end (Figure 153) is often the sign of forthcoming senility. Given the existence of such indicators it might be possible to set up projects or embark on a course of mental exercises which would help to strengthen the mind and thus avoid the effects that such mental weakening would imply.

CHAPTER TWELVE

Careers, Professions, Hobbies and Skills

A good analysis of the hand is, to my mind, invaluable when it comes to career guidance. Helping to steer children in the right direction according to their abilities is a most satisfying job. But what is far more valuable is detecting their hidden talents — gifts which, without some prompting or encouragement, could remain latent or dormant forever. There are those who are late developers, who don't get into their stride until after adolescence, who undertake a course of education totally unsuited to their future capacity and ability. It is through hand analysis that factors such as these can be picked out at a very early age, thus avoiding any future anxieties to which a mistaken course of action might lead.

Guidance and occupational advice can, in the same way, be given throughout the career. Major decisions regarding changes of jobs or professions, crises at work, power struggles, problems with colleagues or superiors, the question of retirement and many, many more issues connected with the individual's working life can be clarified through hand analysis. In addition, hand analysis can also provide advance warning of the possibility of such occurrences well in advance of them actually taking place.

Information, too, regarding talents which can be channelled into hobbies or spare-time activities can be highlighted. This is so much more useful than is immediately apparent when one considers the current unemployment situation and the need to develop oneself within one's leisure time. Indeed, redundancy has enabled many to turn a spare-time pursuit into a successful business. Equally, the development of a latent talent could be the saviour of someone who is stuck at home all day, either because of domestic responsibilities, ill health, unemployment or whatever, and in some cases it can also provide a useful addition to the household budget.

By running through the four levels outlined below and superimposing all the information collected, it is possible to work out the suitability of career, job prospects, latent talents and the general progress of an individual's working life.

Level 1: Hand Shapes

Each basic type of hand, because of the character and personality it represents, is more suited to certain jobs than to others. Bear in mind, though, when applying the basic principles that the shape of the hand may not conform to the pure type but may, indeed, be a combination of several different types and this means that the person concerned may fit into a much broader spectrum than at first appeared. Remember, too, that each level modifies the whole so that the complete pattern of the working life doesn't emerge until each piece of information has been collected and overlaid one on top of the other. Shapes of hands can be checked in Chapter 4, 'Working from a Print'.

The square
Square-handed people are perhaps the hardest workers amongst us. They are practical and down-to-earth, preferring to plod along in a routine way. Anything that takes them out of doors is for them preferable by far to being cooped up in a stuffy office all day long. Because of their earthy nature, these people make very contented farmers, gardeners or anything that takes them close to the soil. The logical pragmatism that some of them display could happily take them into banking or accountancy. For others who incline more towards discipline, law and order, anything connected with the police force, or indeed with the armed forces, would suit. Taking into account the fact that they like to work in a rather systematized way then they, of all people, would be able to cope with any job of a routine or repetitive nature, such as factory work.

The conic
The conic-handed folk tend to be creative and need a lot of variety in their lives. They are lively types who are stimulated by challenge

of all sorts. Excellent with people, they are best working as part of a team in an open, flexible atmosphere where the free exchange of news and views buzzes around everywhere. They are extremely quick learners and catch on very fast indeed. These people make good businessmen and women because they have a knack for organization and are able to make snappy, instinctive judgements and decisions. They are equally good in the secretarial/commercial worlds. Because of their creative turn of mind they may be found in the artistic world, being successful designers or artists, in the world of fashion and especially in the media. Their love of working with people and with ideas takes them not only into the arts but also into humanities and they are excellent when it comes to languages. In fact, any occupation that keeps them busy and on their toes, such as the catering trade, or anything requiring a creative flair, such as dressmaking or hairdressing, would suit.

The spatulate

People with spatulate hands are active, whether mentally or physically, and always seem to have lots of pent-up energy. They are the inventors and pioneers amongst us so any work which requires an inventive and innovative mind would be ideal for them. Science, technology or engineering would all attract these people. Academics, including college and university lecturers, often seem to have spatulate hands. Because they are the builders amongst us, the construction industries would also be suitable for them. Anything of a risky or adventurous nature seems to grab their enthusiasm and they have been known as the explorers or pioneers, in both the real and metaphorical sense. Those spatulates, whose hands are very broad and fleshy at the base of the palm, tend to channel their energies into sports. This is a rather 'masculine' hand so they may be more commonly found in anything normally associated with the male-dominated preserves, such as the navy, for example.

The psychic

The long, sensitive psychic hand belongs to those who tend to be unpredictable and impractical when it comes to worldly affairs. They are the dreamers who have a strong appreciation of beauty and aesthetics. Really, the psychic hand belongs to the poets and fine artists of this world. And, if they don't actually practise the arts themselves, they certainly have a tremendous appreciation for them. Novelists, too, who live in the realms of fiction and fantasy, would more often than not possess this hand type and the literary world in general would be lost without them. Because they are perceptive, they can also make excellent psychoanalysts. Equally, their sensitivity regarding human nature can turn them into very fine actors, actresses and musicians, whilst their sense of culture and refinement could take them into the beauty trade or anything connected with the world of glamour.

Level 2: The Head Line

The next step is to look at the head line because this is the indicator of intellectual abilities and it reveals not only how individuals think but also what they think about. When it comes to career guidance a mere glance at this line reveals the general area the subject is suited to, whether the inclination is more towards the Arts or to the Sciences. The ability to pick out this simple but fundamental difference could be of crucial importance, for example, to youngsters who have to make decisions at a very early age regarding their educational future.

The straighter the line, the more practical, down-to-earth and logical the mentality. This is the sort of mind that applies itself to the more rational, materialistic and concrete subjects. That is why anything connected with business, science, commerce or technology would suit the owners of this sort of line. At work, in their leisure pursuits and even in conversation, such people tend to stick to factual matters for they are not at all interested in anything of an airy-fairy nature, nor indeed do spiritual or occult matters grab their attention for these subjects are simply not realistic enough for them. People with straight head lines are normally considered to be convergent thinkers.

The shorter and the higher up the line, the more the mind is centred on mundane and materialistic affairs. These are the sorts of people whose interests and conversations revolve around material security and possessions — cars, money, property, holidays — anything that has tangible worth and that can be considered real, as opposed to abstract concepts.

The curved line denotes the artistic, creative and imaginative mind.

These people are more inclined towards the arts, music, literature, languages and communications in general. Mentally, they are much more expansive than those with a straight head line for they are divergent thinkers.

The deeper the curve, the more extreme becomes the imagination. People with head lines that reach down into the mount of Luna should find an outlet for their rich, artistic talents, because if they don't their imagination can become so lurid that it can lead to bouts of moodiness, melancholia and even depression. Anything connected with fine arts or fictional literature would suit here, but the message is to keep a tight rein on that imagination and focus it into useful creative projects.

If the line is straight for part of the time but then curves down through the second half of its course it suggests a combination of the pragmatic and creative way of thinking. People with such a line as this can be equally found in the occupations suitable to both types of line. Often, though, they may initially find it extremely hard to make up their minds about which camp to follow and, sometimes, it's even possible for them to reach a crisis half-way through their career and change course altogether. If, then, those in the out-and-out practical or hard-core scientific fields yearn for a little more creative thought they should seek it through their hobbies or spare-time activities.

Alternatively, if those in the pure artistic line should find that they need more rationalization, something to make them feel that their feet are touching terra firma, they ought to concentrate their spare-time energies on more practical pursuits. In these ways both should find their balance and get enough stimulation for all their intellectual needs. Ideally, though, the best types of jobs for these people are those which combine both the practical and creative in one.

When a head line splits into a fork below the ring finger it is known as the writer's fork. This formation is somewhat unusual and denotes heightened powers of creativity. Anyone with this feature who isn't actively engaged in a creative occupation should consider taking up writing, painting, music or anything of an artistic nature as a hobby.

The Simian line, on a normal hand, always signifies intensity. People with this marking need the sort of work in the type of job that requires them to focus their attention and channel their concentration. Any work which requires variety and divergent thinking is not really for this type of person. Indeed, they can become so obsessional about their work that they should be encouraged to take up a really relaxing pastime to help them unwind.

In terms of length, it is usually considered that the shorter the line, the more materialistic the mentality, whereas the longer it is, the more scope for intellectual thought can be expected. This is not always the case in absolute terms but it holds good as a general rule. Of course, it must be remembered that despite its length, if a head line is broken, faint, islanded or chained it will show a weakening of the intellectual potential inasmuch as worries and problems will lead to a lack of concentration, difficulty in decision-making and, overall, 'cotton-wool' thinking. It is the clear, unbroken line which highlights clarity of thought and a lively, vibrant mentality.

Level 3: The Fate Line

Whilst the shape of the hand and the type of head line suggests the sort of occupation an individual is suited to, the fate line actually reveals what happens through that person's career — the events that are likely to take place and changes which may occur within the occupation. In addition, by checking on how to measure the fate line it is even possible to date precisely those events.

A break anywhere along the line denotes a change within the individual's career. If the line ends and a new section overlaps the old, then whatever change of job is implied has occurred through the individual's own instigation. If a tiny deviation in the course of the line is seen, or if the gap between the two overlapping ends is very slight, then the changes suggested would be small or perhaps there would simply be a change of emphasis, such as a promotion or a side-step within the same company. The wider the gap between the two overlapping ends, the bigger the change. This could suggest taking up a new occupation, possibly involving a major move to another part of the country.

If, however, the line comes to an abrupt halt and the line doesn't continue until higher up, this is an indication that changes within the occupation have been made outside the individual's control. This can often be one of the signs of redundancy and, as such, of obvious value if it is picked up well in advance because then contingency plans can be worked out and put into effect. The resumption of the line shows when the normal working life is taken up again.

When a section of the line is wavy, fragmented or very faint it can indicate a period of vacillation, when the individual is in and out of work or tries out one job after another. When the line consolidates and strengthens, then it can be said that the individual has found direction and purpose not only in occupational matters but also in life.

Any tiny bars cutting through the line signify obstruction or opposition. This might be seen if there is any industrial strife, problems with one's workmates, personality clashes or disagreements with colleagues or bosses. Islands in the line, however, invariably indicate financial difficulties.

By carefully analysing the line after these markings it is possible to tell whether the events have worked out for better or worse. If, for instance, the line should considerably strengthen after a break then it shows that the change has been a positive one. But, if the line is weaker or becomes chained or fragmented then it can be seen that the change has brought added difficulties and complications to the subject. To observe such markings and to be able to anticipate the possible eventualities that they represent is surely an invaluable advantage in life, for it allows one to be better prepared, to plan for the future or to avoid the pitfalls that one might otherwise unwittingly fall into. This advance warning, then, allows individuals to be masters or mistresses of their own careers.

Level 4: Special Markings

There are indeed various markings all over the hand with special significance regarding occupational matters. Such markings don't necessarily mean that certain people are predestined to be in particular jobs but simply that they possess natural talents and skills which make them more suited to some careers than to others. If any of these markings should exist on a hand it is recommended that the gifts or talents represented, if not used in the everyday working life, should be channelled into spare-time or leisure-time activities in order to provide as much satisfaction and fulfilment to that person as possible.

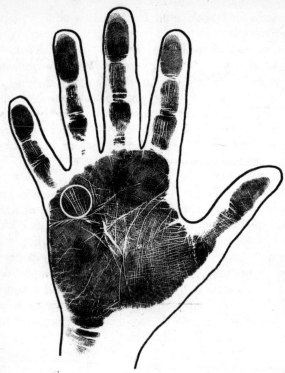

Figure 154

The healing hand

One of the most special markings to look out for on this hand is the medical stigmata which is seen in the hand print illustrated in Figure 154. This formation consists of three vertical lines crossed by a horizontal or oblique one and situated on the palm below the ring and little fingers. People with this formation have a natural gift for healing even if they are not trained in the orthodox medical profession. Indeed, not all doctors or nurses possess the medical stigmata but those who do seem to make the better, more understanding and sympathetic practitioners. Those who have the marking but are not medically trained may like to think about spiritual healing, herbalism or simply working with people in the caring professions such as social workers, child minders or whatever.

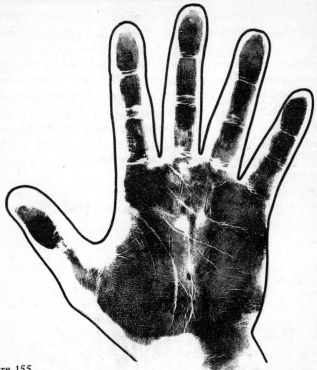

Figure 155

The agriculturalist

It is the square hand which is most associated with farmers and all those connected with the land. Often a long basal phalanx on the middle finger is a good sign of someone who is a keen gardener and who has what is known as 'green fingers'. This feature, if seen on a more creative hand, may indicate the landscape gardener. One especially rare marking which is seen on a few hands is a skin loop entering the palm low down from the percussion side (see Figure 155). This feature denotes a rare sensitivity to, and understanding of, flora and fauna so that those who possess this marking seem to have an inherent rapport with nature.

The craftsman

People who work with their hands may have any of the basic shaped palms but the one feature which makes them stand apart is the angularity at the base of the thumb which is known as the angle of manual dexterity. Another factor to watch out for amongst these people, whether they are carpenters, do-it-yourself experts, people who work in handicrafts or whatever, is that those who possess long fingers will probably take much longer over their work than the shorter-fingered types, but they are likely to be much more methodical and painstaking. So, if a job needs to be done quickly and perhaps with not too much precision but with plenty of inspiration, then go for the short-fingered folk in this category. But, if absolute precision and accuracy is required, then the longer-fingered person would be better.

Teachers and academics
Teachers may have any of the basic shaped hands, but the one

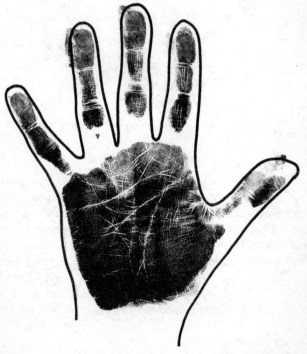

Figure 156

outstanding feature that marks out those with a special gift for imparting information is known as the 'teacher's square' (see Figure 156). This is a formation consisting of four tiny lines formed into a square and it is found lying below the index finger. Those with this feature but who are not in the teaching profession may find that they are able to instruct or explain to others with great ease and they often derive much pleasure in teaching their own children. Many lecturers seem to have the spatulate shaped hand and the longer the top phalanges of the fingers, the more intellectual the individual. An extremely long top phalanx on the middle finger highlights those who love research and a noticeably tapered basal phalanx on that same finger denotes the perpetual student, someone who takes great delight in always learning new things. If all the joints of the fingers are pronounced, other than through illness or injury, then this is known as the philosophical hand and as such represents the hand of the thinker.

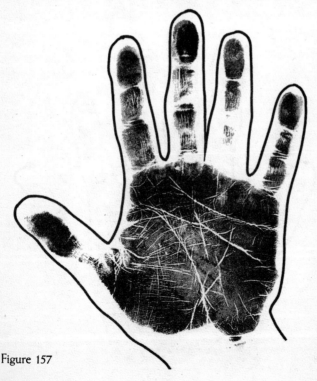

Figure 157

The sporty hand

People who are involved in active sports invariably have very strong, muscular hands (see Figure 157). The seat of energy, or the power-house, is located at the base of the palm so that if the lower mounts of Venus and Luna are well-developed then the individual has plenty of vitality and physical stamina. It is this development at the base of the palm which characterizes the active sportsman. Women who play sports, though, may not have this sort of strength portrayed but may, alternatively, have rather wiry hands which would signify fitness and robustness.

The creative hand

One of the instantly recognizable signs of the creative hand is the bowed percussion. A bowed head line, too, reveals an imaginative, expansive and divergent mentality. If the fingers are short on the creative hand

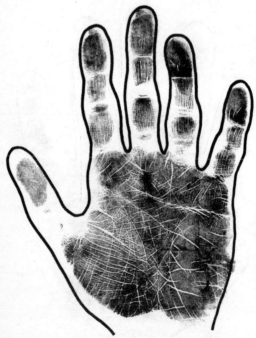

Figure 158

then there will be instinctive and inspirational flair, as portrayed in Figure 158 which is the print of a young and highly talented designer. But, if the fingers are long, then methodical, painstaking work is more the order of the day. The angle of manual dexterity will also highlight those who enjoy working with their hands.

The armed forces

The square or spatulate hand would be the most suitable when considering those in the armed forces as both these have a basic toughness. Characteristically, the mount of Mars should be large or well-developed as this suggests a certain aggressive strength. Amongst them, the leaders of men would be those who have extra-long indices although this in itself can be a sign of the tyrant or dictator. It has been said that both Napoleon and Hitler had longer index fingers than their middle ones.

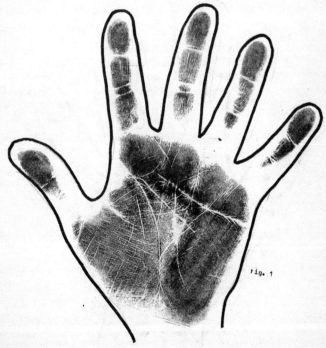

fig. 1

Figure 159

The commercial or secretarial hand

The only hand shape which is definitely not suitable to this category would be the psychic one. Both the straight and curved head lines would fit — the first denoting practical and logical application whilst the second would add a certain flair with the general public. Figure 159 provides an example of the hand print of a most efficient and successful private secretary.

The good cook

The hands of cooks and caterers are typified by full, podgy, basal phalanges on all the fingers but especially so on the index, as seen in Figure 160 which is the print of an excellent Italian cook who makes the most wonderful pasta dishes ever tasted! If this latter phalanx is

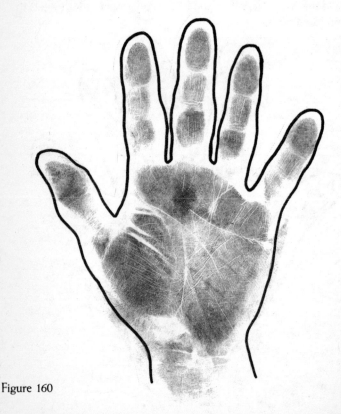

Figure 160

somewhat longer and, although full, is firm, then it would suggest the gourmet and often restaurateurs have this feature prominently displayed in their hands. The good housekeeper, and equally, the person who can 'stretch a pound to a fiver', is marked out by long second phalanges on the fingers as this denotes efficiency and an excellent sense of management.

CHAPTER THIRTEEN

The Unforeseen

There is no doubt that one of the most positive advantages of hand analysis is that is provides a glimpse into possible future events and occurrences. Although it must be stressed that such indications are not absolute, it must still be, nevertheless, of greater benefit to have a hint of their likelihood than not to know at all. Armed with such knowledge, we are able to anticipate, to make contingency plans, to prepare ourselves and possibly even deflect or prevent altogether, if necessary, anything untoward from happening. On the plus side, this sort of predictive information can also help to encourage or confirm our decisions for the future.

The common fallacy that the lines on our hands never change and that consequently we are stuck with what we are born with is, at last, being put to rights. Lines can change for a number of reasons according to our decisions; changes in our way of life, experiences, state of health and even our diets can have a direct influence on them. If we had no powers of intervention, no control over our lives, then we would be mere puppets in the hands of the gods. And if so, then what would be the point of learning, of growing, of developing our minds?

Certainly it can be said that we do not have absolute control but that we are able to choose from a limited selection according to our disposition and circumstances. But, even if this is the case, then we should be empowered to make the best possible decisions within our scope. Without the full realization of the consequences of our actions and decisions, not only upon our own lives but also on the lives of those around us, we cannot be expected to make such choices with clarity and confidence. Often it is only with hindsight that we can appreciate the whole picture, whereas through an analysis of our hands we are able to see the patterns of events, the possible ripples and ramifications of our future before us.

It is the fact that we all have free will that allows us that degree of control. If, for instance, we saw that an emotional upheaval was likely to loom on the horizon we would at least have certain options in the way we could deal with its eventuality. Rather than blindly fall into that sort of event, we might be able to modify the circumstances so that its impact would not be so great. Perhaps it could even be possible to skirt around it altogether or, if it were totally unavoidable, then at least we could brace ourselves and thus be prepared to handle it.

It is rather like a doctor who advises his patient that if he continues to smoke sixty cigarettes a day, he would very likely find himself in a wheelchair in five years' time. If, however, he gives up now, his health would have time to recuperate. Such an individual might show the signs of impending ill health in his hand in, say, a large island on the life line. Should he, on that medical advice, subsequently give up, then there would be an excellent chance for that island to disappear and for the line to regain its strength.

The hand, then, can be thought of as a map of our conscious and subconscious processes. It is a map which is constantly being modified as we go through life. Just as the ravages of time can be seen on an individual's face, so too, do events, experiences and influences leave their mark on our hands.

It is one thing to appreciate why our own experiences should be shown in our hands but it is quite another to accept that external influences, events occurring to others which touch our own lives, should also be marked there too. We could perhaps imagine that our hands are like photographic plates which receive and imprint our own ideas, actions and decisions and that, whether consciously or subconsciously, we have a certain awareness of the implications and consequences of these upon our future lives. This sort of theory would explain why future indications, both of the negative and positive kinds, are engraved in our palms.

But how much more difficult it is to explain, and then to accept, that sudden, unexpected events which are outside our sphere of influence should also be imprinted in our hands. Consider the example of being able to predict that an individual is likely to be suddenly made redundant in, say, three years' time. How is it possible to explain that that person could have the sort of precognitive knowledge necessary to make the corresponding markings in his or her hand? Well, perhaps one way of explaining this kind of phenomenon is through Jung's concept of the collective unconscious — the notion that we are all in some way mentally interconnected through our ancestral experiences. Or perhaps the concept of the Zeitgeist — the idea that we can all pick up the prevailing trends, the thoughts and feelings of our times — might suit the explanation better.

However the phenomenon occurs, there is no doubt but that it does occur. So, when analysing a hand, look out for some of the future indications which are outlined below. In this way the unexpected or the unforeseen no longer remains the unknown threat but rather becomes an advanced warning which can then be treated as a challenge and so dealt with accordingly.

Emotional Upheavals

Emotional upsets of one sort or another are represented by long horizontal or oblique lines originating from the mounts of Mars or Venus and which then proceed to cross the life line. These are known as trauma lines and the event can be timed at the very point where

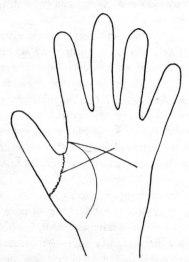

Figure 161

the line crosses the life line. The longer and bolder the line, often cutting right across the head, fate and heart lines, the more impact that upset has upon the subject. It is the origin of the line which reveals the source of the upheaval. If it begins from, or near, the family ring, as demonstrated in Figure 161, then the problems will be centred around parents and close family relations. If the line springs from a relationship line, inside the life line, then it will be that influence or that person who is responsible for the unhappiness.

This sort of event may also have its repercussions on the head line. An island occurring at the same time would indicate the consequent worry and anxiety felt by the individual. If a dip is seen in the head line, or even the tiniest dropped branch, then the result of such emotional trauma would be a marked period of depression. Again, how long this period is likely to last can be timed on the head line.

The sad loss or bereavement of a beloved partner may sometimes be registered by an exceptionally long 'marriage line' which runs right across, below the Mercury and Apollo fingers, and drops down to cut the heart line and possibly even the fate line too.

Moves and Changes of Life-Style

Changes of residence may be denoted by tiny dropped branches off the life line (Figure 162a). Travel or important journeys are also marked in this way but in these cases the branches may be somewhat longer in length. The very deeply etched branches which are seen shooting out towards the Luna mount from the bottom third of the life line may indicate major moves after middle age. Sometimes this can suggest a new life for one's retirement, sometimes even retirement abroad if the line is especially long and strong reaching right into the Luna mount.

A life line which seems to terminate but which is, in fact, overlapped by a brand new section is indicative of a completely new way of life. The wider the gap between the overlapping ends, the greater the difference in life-style. Should the new section begin further out towards the centre of the palm then the life becomes much wider, much more active. But, if the new section begins inside the life line, that is, towards the thumb, then it is possible that the new life is more restricted, more limited than the former one. Always check that what appears at first sight to be a very short line may, in fact, be just a section of the whole

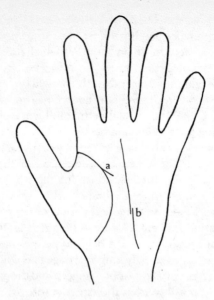

Figure 162

line which is connected by a fine thread to the next section lying further away in the palm. Such a formation would, of course, denote a completely new environment and a completely new way of life.

In the same way, any overlapping breaks in the fate line also reveal changes in the way of life but, because the indications are on this line, these changes may be directly caused by occupational matters (Figure 162b).

All these changes can be dated on both the life and fate lines.

Influences, Relationships and Marriage

Influence lines are seen rising from the mount of Luna towards the fate line. Strong lines show the important relationships affecting the individual. But, if the line is fragmented, islanded or chained then the influence is said to be difficult or unfavourable. If one of these strong branches should actually unite with the fate line, that is usually recognized as a marriage or, at least, as the time when the relationship consolidates itself. If, however, the rising branch falls short of merging into the fate line, or if it cuts right across it, then the relationship is

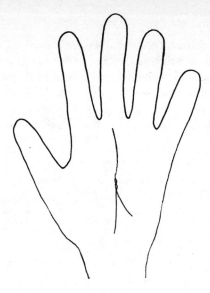

Figure 163

likely to end unhappily. This sort of formation is seen when, for instance, a wedding is called off right at the last moment.

If, after the merger, the fate line is strong and solid, then the relationship or marriage has a noticeably positive effect on the individual. In the cases where the fate line grows thinner or chained after the union (Figure 163), then it is likely that the relationship brings much difficulty with it. When, after the merger, the fate line ends and a new section begins, this tells that the marriage marks the start of a new life for that individual, possibly implying a major move or a change of job.

Occasionally, a branch rising from the Luna mount may not actually touch the fate line at all but proceeds to follow parallel to it. In this example the relationship is an exceptionally good one and regarded more as a partnership than a marriage.

Lines running parallel to the inside of the life line can also represent relationships and influences. But small branches which shoot out of the line itself towards the thumb side may denote offspring.

All these events and indications can be measured off against the main lines of fate and life.

Opposition and Interference

Bars which cut across the main lines are known as opposition or interference lines. Small bars cutting the life line show obstacles in the individual's path. Those cutting the head line denote temporary worries and anxieties which act like little setbacks. Across the fate line, these bars can indicate problems at work, frustrations, trouble with bosses or colleagues or general hiccups in the normal course of the working life.

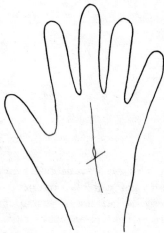

Figure 164

It is the quality of the main line after the crossing bar that shows the sort of effect the opposition has had on the individual. If the main line continues unhampered then the influence was only transient, but if the line should then break, develop an island (Figure 164) or thin out, it can be said that the interference has had a detrimental effect on the individual.

Personal Successes

The most usual way for personal success to be registered is by a rising branch. This formation may shoot up from any of the main lines of head life or fate.

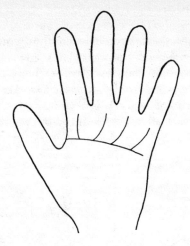

Figure 165

From the head line (Figure 165) the rising branch would indicate a mental achievement and its emphasis lies in whichever area its direction takes. To Jupiter would indicate academic accomplishments. To Saturn signifies career advancement or possibly sometimes success in property deals. To Apollo reveals artistic or creative fulfilment and satisfaction. To Mercury has several interpretations but mainly it would convey successful business or financial deals. Alternatively, this could indicate scientific or even literary advancements.

Branches rising upwards from the body of the life line have the same implications but these suggest that the achievements are as a direct result of the individual's personal efforts and endeavours.

Again, those seen rising from the fate line may be interpreted in the same way and this time the achievements implied would specifically apply to the individual's career and way of life.

All these indications can be timed on the main lines thus opening up the subject's mind to future opportunities and encouraging work and effort in the areas indicated.

Occupational Changes

Changes of job or career are normally marked on the fate line. A long, strong line which begins at the wrist and shoots right up to the Saturn mount, without any breaks or deviation of course, suggests a life spent in the same job, with the same company or firm, from leaving school right through to retirement. This sort of line used to be more common in the 'following in father's footsteps' days or when changes of job and social mobility were not possible options in a worker's life. Quite the opposite to this is a line which is broken up and fragmented as this denotes constant vacillations, being in and out of jobs, and a lack of firm direction.

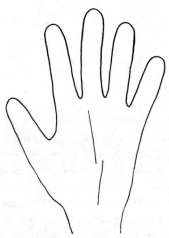

Figure 166

Generally, changes in direction, overlapping sections or complete breaks in the line correspond to changes within the working life. The slightest change of direction detected in the line can indicate modifications in the career, either a promotion, a side-step or different responsibilities. Two overlapping sections reveal a change of occupation, usually prompted by the individual. If the ends have a wide space in between (Figure 166), then the change is a big one and might also imply a move or a different life-style. Where the fate line suddenly comes to an abrupt end this marks the likelihood of a redundancy or the sudden termination of that part of the individual's working life. It is not until the line begins again that the career is resumed. These times can be worked out on the fate line well in advance so that alternative plans can be made to prepare for these contingencies.

It has been said that there are two other warnings on this line regarding occupational affairs. Firstly, if the line suddenly ends on the head line itself, it is considered a warning that a serious misjudgement or miscalculation could radically prejudice or detrimentally affect the career. Secondly, should the fate line terminate on the heart line then it is possible that an emotional indiscretion or *faux pas* could prematurely bring the career to an end.

Future Health Trends

Indications of possible future ill health or well-being may be detected all over the hand. The first areas to investigate, when considering this aspect, are the finger tips. Horizontal lines developing here indicate the onset of stress and worry which should be dealt with, possibly through relaxation techniques, before the anxieties take their toll on the whole physiological system. Should more horizontal dashes be seen on the objective hand than on the subjective, then the problems are just beginning. When both sets of finger tips display the same amount of marking, the individual is at the height of the crisis but, once there are more lines on the subjective hand, then the anxieties are being resolved and the worries nearly over.

Vertical lines deeply etching the finger tips may denote some disturbance of the endocrine system although much more research needs to be done in this field. A concentration of these lines, though, on the tip of the little finger does seem, I have found, to point to certain thyroid conditions.

The slow onset of disease may be detected by the fading of some of the main lines and, more importantly, by the breaking up of the skin ridges. Some rheumatic conditions together with the build-up of acidity in the system (Figure 167), for instance, may be seen in this way on the percussion edge of the palm.

Islands on the life line can warn of impending weakness of one sort or another. Occurring at the top of the line, these can indicate a predisposition to bronchial, sinusitis, nose or throat problems. Lower down, islands may denote back or spinal trouble. Further down still, these formations can show a general debility or they may simply

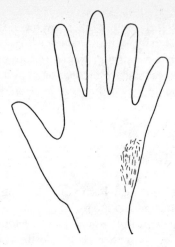

Figure 167

highlight a period of possible ill health.

A series of chaining on the lines, especially on those of heart and head, may reveal that the body chemistry is out of order or that certain mineral deficiencies exist.

The indications of possible accidents or physical injuries can sometimes be spotted on the life line. These may be marked by fine lines rising from the main line up towards the Saturn mount followed by either a break or an island on the life line itself. This, however, must be carefully investigated as a similar formation can mean a change of address or of life-style.

It must be stressed that all these markings are signs or warnings of potential disease or ill health and that, with care and attention, they may never manifest themselves or develop into serious chronic disorders. The hand should be used as a guide to the possible weak links in the subject's physical constitution and not as a direct means of diagnosis. If the subject is indeed uncomfortable or worried about health issues then professional medical advice should be sought.

Personal Fulfilment

Signs of personal fulfilment, contentment and satisfaction may be revealed by the appearance of the Apollo line. It is from the point where this line springs up that true inner happiness or a deep sense of creative fulfilment is felt. The timing on this line may be matched against, and read off, the fate line.

Independent star formations on the Jupiter and Apollo mounts are also excellent auguries of the sort of success which would bring a considerable amount of personal satisfaction with it.

The Totally Unexpected

Events which occur out of the blue and which are totally unexpected may be marked by a star on the fate line (Figure 168). This is invariably a sign of a shock to the system and, although it may not be possible to actually predict the cause of the incident, it nevertheless alerts the individual to be extra careful around the time indicated.

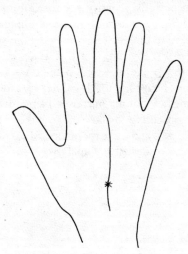

Figure 168

CHAPTER FOURTEEN

An Example Analysis

In this final chapter I should like to illustrate how all the levels discussed are brought together in order to formulate a personal analysis of an individual's hand prints. The analysis I have chosen for this purpose belongs to a lady who came to consult me because she felt that, after a strict Victorian upbringing followed by a disastrous marriage, she had lost all sense of personal identity and direction in life. She had recently been freed from her unfaithful and tyrannical husband and was desperately trying to pick up the pieces. At the age of fifty-nine she wondered if there was anything worthwhile left for her in life and, indeed, if there were any pieces worth picking up at all.

For obvious reasons I have not disclosed her true identity but have used a fictitious name here for my purposes. I am indebted to 'Marcia Gray' not only for consenting to allow me to publish her case-study, but also for so generously, and quite spontaneously, writing to me with a commentary on the results of my analysis.

The Analysis

'Marcia Gray'
Right-handed
b. 23.3.1924

The shape of your palm is a mixture of square to oblong, which indicates that you are basically hard-working, practical and down-to-earth. There is a feeling of solidity and strength here although the oblong features add urbanity and cultured and civilized tastes. Perhaps you tend more towards the urban rather than the rural way of life and you are probably more inclined to indoor pursuits and interests than the more sporty

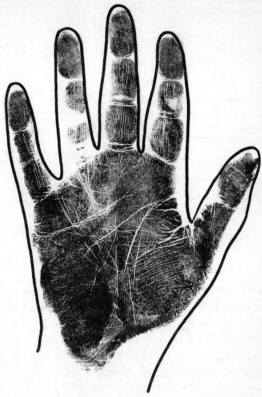

Figure 169a

or outdoor hobbies. Certainly there is balance, symmetry seen here with a delicate, discriminating eye, a preference for quality rather than quantity. The Luna mount is full and low-set, which highlights your deep sensitivity and receptivity to moods and atmosphere. You are endowed with much creative potential and a rich and fertile imagination. This suggests a primal sort of sensitivity showing that you have the potential for psychism and even a touch of clairvoyance. Moreover, this sensitivity can manifest itself in a rapport with nature, with flora and fauna and with the natural rhythms of the earth. When it comes to people, this indicates an ability to readily understand, sympathize and empathize with others.

The mounts of Mars are both large and full. One denotes strong physical courage, tenacity and perseverance in the face of adversity

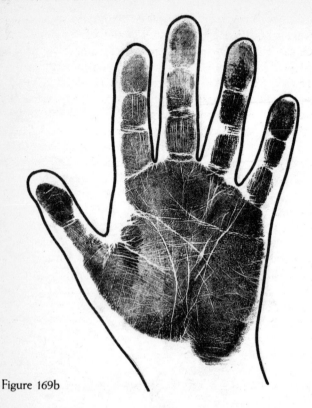

Figure 169b

and the other reveals moral courage, strength of your own convictions, loyalty to your friends and loved ones and a feeling that you don't easily turn your back on those who need you. The whole of the ulna side of your palm is more developed than the radial side, with the percussion edge significantly bowed. This prominence reveals that your intuition is supreme and probably one of your greatest assets. There is more than a touch of prescience here with plenty of insight and foresight. You are also likely to have vivid and prophetic dreams especially so in times of trouble. The Jupiter mount is prominent in your hand and illustrates a social conscience — an awareness of your environment and a concern for environmental issues.

The fingers are slightly short in comparison to the palms and this shortness reflects inspiration, intuition, a quick lively mind that catches on at a glance, that learns easily, especially from past mistakes, and picks things up swiftly. Perhaps, too, there's a touch of restless mental energy for there's certainly a degree of impatience, particularly so with stupidity and minutiae. You are the sort who likes making plans, thinking up new ideas and getting new projects off the ground. The Jupiter fingers are held in a straight and upright position which in you denotes honesty, responsibility and forthrightness. The stance of your fingers is most interesting as there is a discrepancy between right and left. On the right, the 2nd and 3rd fingers have a tendency to open out slightly more so than on the left. Firstly, this immediately suggests that you are becoming more resourceful and self-sufficient. Secondly, the stance here shows that more and more you are finding that you need to be on your own, either so that you can work quietly without interruptions and distractions or because you need to recharge your batteries, to take stock of your situation, as it were, commune with nature or simply be on your own for a while. The stance of our fingers can change according to our circumstances so this could indeed be a temporary state for you when you are 'taking time out' or simply 'licking your wounds' and indeed it would seem to be a very natural thing for you to do after such a long time of emotional upheaval. Needless to say, the configuration of your fingers can change again when you start to regain your inner strength, when you recreate your trust in the world and slowly start to feel that you can comfortably relate to others on your own terms again. Everything about your hand indicates that this is not too far away.

The longest phalanx on your fingers is the top one on the ring finger and this usually signifies a strong creative and artistic streak and it denotes an intellectual approach to the arts in general. Notice how the little fingers are bent, particularly so the left one. This tells that you are the sort who would sacrifice your own dreams, aims and ambitions for the sake of those you love. For instance, you would be prepared to give up a good job if you felt that your family needed you at home, for you always put others before yourself. This denotes a wonderful, caring and altruistic nature, but you must be aware that this self-sacrificial disposition can all too often be taken advantage of, abused or completely outgrown by those upon whom you lavish your attention. So whatever you do, you must keep a little corner in your activities for yourself either in the form of a hobby or interest in which you can excel or make into your own special forte. On top of this, the little finger is also very low set in relation to the rest of the fingers and this suggests that, probably because of a strict and restricted childhood coupled with marital difficulties, you have simply had your self-confidence knocked out of you. What you must remember is that this is not a negative character trait intrinsic in your nature but that circumstances have led you to lack faith in yourself and in your abilities, to feel uncertain about yourself and your powers of self-expression. In fact, your hand is a much gifted one which has not been given the opportunity to flourish and to blossom in its own right and in order to redress this imbalance you should find yourself a subject which really interests you and in which you can excel so that you can boost your confidence in yourself whilst immersing yourself in something totally absorbing.

Much of this is also reflected by the fact that you possess somewhat short thumbs and this may mean that at times you have felt that events just take over and you are compelled to go along with the flow rather than take the lead or initiative yourself. With your new growing inner strength, however, you should find it much easier to take control of prevailing situations yourself. The thumb is, nevertheless, very well-shaped and well-proportioned so you are a well-balanced person with good powers of reason and logic. The second phalanx of the thumb is fine and waisted, indicating discretion, tact and diplomacy. Both thumbs are held at an acute angle, so you are quiet and reserved, with perhaps a few inhibitions, and through hardships of one kind or another you have learnt to be resilient and determined. This also indicates that you are rather tense, which is not surprising, but which is possibly limiting your outlook on life. Do beware of not becoming too 'closed' or too independent for you must find time to unwind and to loosen up mentally, physically and emotionally. If you could practise some mental relaxation and tension release exercises you should find that in a short while you would feel considerably more relaxed and flexible. As your hand displays that you have manual dexterity, you must be adept at any work which requires nimble fingers, anything to do with craftwork, making things, etc. you might consider absorbing yourself with these types of pursuits as a form of relaxing and stimulating pastime.

Your finger prints are a mixture of loop, whorl and arch patterns. The majority are loops, which emphasizes your adaptability and the gift of being able to make the best out of any situation. This also indicates the graceful mind, a desire to learn and to find new ideas. The arches on your second fingers reveal a certain idealism, particularly where politics and religion are concerned. The whorl on your right Apollo finger essentially enhances your creativity whereas that on the right thumb shows strength of character, determination and even stubbornness. It is possible that, given this formation, other people may at times experience you as slow in giving your reactions and in reaching a decision but in fact the reason for this is because you simply need time in order to process information and to arrive at your own conclusions.

There is one last interesting pattern which must be explained and this is a low formation of rings lying at the base of the Apollo finger. Here, the pattern suggests a tinge of pessimism in your character and it is the sort of pessimism which rears its head when you are at your happiest or when things are going particularly well. At those times you can't believe your good fortune and you expect that something will inevitably come along to shatter your happiness. That very expectation makes you look around and find something to upset you. I have seen this time and time again with people who have this marking and what you are in fact doing is fulfilling your own prophesies. Perhaps at those times, if you were to think positively, to expect that you are entitled to good times and to happiness then maybe you wouldn't mar your own joy.

Your whole hand appears neat, tidy and compact, thus reflecting your own character. The head line is bowed, again highlighting a creative and imaginative turn of mind. At its beginning it is heavily intermeshed with the life line and this always tells of discord and disharmony during the early years. So, in your case it would suggest that you were perhaps held back and there were overtones of worries and anxieties throughout your childhood. The lines clear towards your late teens but there is still that indication of imposed control and it wasn't until your mid 20s (24-25) when you seemed at last to free yourself from those early influences. At that very point a branch rises towards the heart line so you must have regarded the new independence as an emotional achievement at that time. By around 36 a strong branch is dropped from the head line indicating a time of emotional upheaval, so much so that it left you feeling quite depressed. By around 41 a tiny shoot shows signs of encouragement as this denotes mental achievement and a sense of expansion and growth. Once into your mid 40s, though, the line becomes a little fuzzy. This indicates a period when you were not intellectually at your best — your thinking might have been somewhat confused, unclear, decisions difficult to make. The whole effect is rather cotton-woolly and indeed this condition continues through the rest of your 40s and even becomes more exacerbated throughout most of your 50s.

Interestingly, the left head line displays an unusual construction during this time. At around 48 a new section of line develops under the original line and by your later 50s surpasses it and completely takes over from the old one. This suggests that from your late 40s you developed quite a new kind of mental awareness, almost like a rebirth: you must have started to question your beliefs, your ideas about life, you began to review your emotions, your aims and your desires. It was a period of change, of intellectual growth and expansion, a time when, basically you sorted yourself out. The new section has been growing stronger since your mid 50s, highlighting that this new mental stance, this new perspective in life has been giving you enormous intellectual strength and comfort and, by around 57 when the new line has completely superseded the old, it tells how you have broken away from your former self and how much more positive you have become and so able to stand on your own two feet.

On the right hand, the head line is almost transformed once you turn from your 50s into your 60s. Then, your new decade sees the line becoming fine again, the fuzziness disappears and with it heralds clarity of thought and a sharper mind. As the line bows more positively down towards the Luna mount it suggests heightened powers of imagination and creative thought, a generally more relaxed approach to life and especially so from your mid 60s onwards. It is possible that the transition from your 50s to your 60s may not be completely smooth, as periods of transition often cause the individual to be restless, unsure and strained. So make sure that you don't over-tax yourself, that you take care of your health and that you don't let things get on top of you. You have so much to look forward to, as the rest of the hand reveals, so try to relax and not to mourn for what is past but look to your future as a golden age of rebirth.

The trends seen on the head line are reflected in the life line. Age

26 was highlighted as a complete change in your way of life at that time. Age 30 is significantly marked as a time of personal achievement through your own efforts and hard work. Despite this, though, a lot of underlying tension, interference and setbacks are implied by several trauma bars crossing the main life line. Ages 33 and 36 are even more noticeable — the latter date indicating a profound reversal and perhaps marking one of the most important emotional upsets of your life.

The life line, however, continues to be assailed by bars crossing the mounts from the thumb and this denotes constant pressures and worries connected with your loved ones and your domestic situation. In fact, this all seems to come to the boil towards your late 40s when a loyalty crease stretches right out and touches the main line. Here it would appear that your very loyalty was brought into question when you must have felt torn between your emotions and rational judgement of your circumstances at that time. This coincides with the development of the new section of head line on your left hand and marks the time when your whole new approach to life was sparked off. A branch is dropped from the line at around 55 which often signifies a change, a move, a new house or some important turning point in your life. The left line actually ends at this point; it branches and swings out towards the centre of the palm, so it was indeed a significant event which was to lead to a whole new way of life.

At present another similar branch is about to shoot out so it is likely that, unless you have already just moved, another new change is imminent. Around your 60th year the changeover process should be complete. From then on, the life line continues smoothly on its way, unhampered by interference lines thus suggesting a much more stable time with ensuing greater peace of mind.

It is the fate line and more particularly the Apollo line which, together, augur so much good for the future. Notice how the fate line was fragmented and broken up between the ages of 36 and 55. This fragmentation depicts a lack of direction, frustration, limitations and interference of one sort or another throughout those 19-20 years. When a fate line is thus broken up it's as if the individual were not in control of his/her own destiny but at the mercy of the prevailing circumstances or environment. This, then is the picture portrayed by your hand and, as revealed by the other major lines, it was not until the latter half of your 50s that the line picked up again with renewed strength and vigour so that at last you began to regain control of your own helm, as it were, to feel mistress of your own fate. Yet again, we see new commencements, new beginnings with the growth of a brand new section of fate line towards the very end of your 50s and the beginning of your 60s and this is echoed by the brilliant presence of the Apollo lines suddenly rising at this point. The impact of these lines should reverberate right through every aspect of your life for their appearance denotes an inner feeling of contentment, of satisfaction and even of well-being. Rising as they do above the heart line, they are classically an indication of the growth of happiness in one's later years accompanied by a sense of creative fulfilment and often much mutual sympathy, affection and understanding from friendships and close relationships.

Your hand does indeed show that you have a good deal to look forward to in life. Transition periods are, needless to say, difficult at the best of times and, it must be remembered, that you are going through a period of readjustment where you are picking up the pieces and restructuring your life after more than twenty years of uncertainty about yourself and your abilities. Do believe in yourself and allow yourself to be guided by your inner instincts and powers of intuition, with which you are so richly endowed judging by the rare marking of a bow of intuition which you possess. Immerse yourself in as many creative and challenging pursuits as you can, as this should lead to much satisfaction in the not too distant future.

September 1983

The Commentary, by 'Marcia Gray'

Those who have found the analysis of my hand interesting will also be interested I am sure, in the commentary which I offered to make for Lori Reid as a mark of my esteem for her professional skills and powers of perception.

The analysis which she has made is remarkably accurate in its understanding of my character and personality and even more remarkable in the pinpointing of dates which were of great importance in my life.

I was so impressed by her own personality and commitment to her work, that from the day I received her analysis I restructured my life to follow the paths she had indicated. As she does not make predictions, but reveals the pointers already in the hand, it was less difficult to accept these 'leader' lines, than a predictive horoscope for example. The restructuring meant turning away from intended paths, but there can be no question that this has proved to be the right way for my future development.

The revelation that intuition is shown as a strong asset caused me to pay attention to flashes of insight instead of dismissing these as 'imagination'. This has been helpful in many difficult situations and has avoided problems which might otherwise have arisen.

Also, the recognition of the faults of impatience has brought awareness of the need for more sensitivity in dealings with others: the knowledge of an inclination towards independence and self-sufficiency — which could lead to selfishness — has been valuable in preventing this unpleasant trait from developing. These were warning lights which were a guide for my behaviour towards others.

I was greatly impressed by the revelation of past difficulties which have in effect been a blight on my life. Having attention drawn to talents and character traits which are worth developing but which have, in the past been ignored, has given me the enthusiasm to explore and pursue these talents, which are now a major factor in the policy of new development and growth.

Experiments with numerous skills and activities giving scope for creative development are meeting with increasing success in both artistic and literary fields. Increasing confidence based on the knowledge of myself gained from Mrs Reid's analysis, is a key factor in this development.

To know that one actually has the talent and ability to do certain things is a powerful influence, and encourages perseverance where, previously, one had easily been deflated, or deflected, by the belief of the innate inability to succeed in particular fields.

The ages at which events of great importance have occurred are again accurate. For someone who had never met me — a total stranger to me — it is disconcerting to know that my life can be read from my palm, as Mrs Reid has revealed. This only increases my acceptance of her readings as everything can be checked.

At the age of 26 my life changed completely.

At 30 I founded my own highly successful business and became one of the highest-paid female executives in the country.

From 33 to 36, family difficulties, ending in tragic bereavement, caused deep and lasting trauma.

In my mid 40s a painful decision forced me to give up my business and go to live elsewhere. The choice of family or business — the usual dilemma forced upon women. Convention prevailed and family commitments won. The comment made by Mrs Reid, 'that I must have felt torn between emotions and rational judgement', is so perceptive and true.

At the age of 48, I became involved with a political movement which did change my thinking and attitudes of a lifetime. It was undoubtedly a period of growth and mental expansion.

At 54 another significant change of course took place. Leaving a beloved home and moving to a strange and uncongenial area and environment to live as a widow. This was a completely new life without the support of a loved partner, and very much at 'the mercy of prevailing circumstances and the environment'.

It was these circumstances which sent me in desperation to Lori Reid. Her brilliant analysis has now become my guide and mentor. Not only have I found new knowledge of myself, but, following her guidance, I have sought out the talents bestowed upon me, and have used them to good purpose.

She has helped to take control of my life and to do this with more care for others than I might previously have done.

Most important, she has revealed to me, my own life, as it has been influenced by my own actions, and also by the actions of those who were in a position to influence me and my development. A late developer now, I hope to prove that it is never really too late, and my life is brighter and more hopeful than it has been for many years.

It is to express the gratitude that I feel to Mrs Reid that I have given my consent to the use of my analysis for publication in her book. It was not an easy decision. Such sensitive and private revelations are not intended for publication when consultations are arranged. But she has brought so many benefits to my own life that I have overcome any natural reluctance and have volunteered this commentary in the hope that anyone reading it will learn that with guidance, it is possible to enhance life and grow at whatever age we are. The map written in every hand, correctly interpreted, is that guide towards a happy and fulfilled future.

I do wish Lori Reid's book every success and her readers a better understanding of the factors which influence their lives.

May 1984

INDEX

Books of further interest:

LIFE LINES
A NEW INTRODUCTION TO PALMISTRY

Peter West. *Fully illustrated.* Popular introductory guide to palmistry, written by an expert palmist who regularly contributes to *Prediction* magazine. Learn how to assess character, talent and potential, detect illness! Written in the light of modern research, the author's twenty-five years of experience, the book explains: Study of the hand shape; Study of palm features, particularly the lines; Study of the palm surface and skin patterns of the fingers. There is also a chapter on hand gesture, an inexhaustible source of information, which enables a palmist to define certain character traits within the personality.

THE PALMISTRY WORKBOOK
UNDERSTANDING THE ART OF PSYCHOLOGICAL HAND ANALYSIS

Nathaniel Altman. *Illustrated.* The first systematic manual for decoding and interpreting the secret language of our hands. The product of 15 years of research and practical experience, it shows how to analyse the hand for enlightenment on a wide range of subjects including love, relationships and sexuality, health, career guidance and self-fulfilment, spiritual life. Clear, authoritative, and completely up-to-date, this book is an indispensable practical guide to psychological hand analysis — the *only* book you ever need on this fascinating subject.